First World War
and Army of Occupation
War Diary
France, Belgium and Germany

62 DIVISION
Divisional Troops
Royal Army Veterinary Corps
2/1 West Riding Mobile Veterinary Section
9 November 1916 - 30 August 1919

WO95/3078/4

The Naval & Military Press Ltd
www.nmarchive.com
Published in association with The National Archives

Published by

The Naval & Military Press Ltd

Unit 10 Ridgewood Industrial Park,

Uckfield, East Sussex,

TN22 5QE England

Tel: +44 (0) 1825 749494

www.naval-military-press.com

www.nmarchive.com

This diary has been reprinted in facsimile from the original. Any imperfections are inevitably reproduced and the quality may fall short of modern type and cartographic standards.

© **Crown Copyright**
Images reproduced by permission of The National Archives, London, England, 2015.

Contents

Document type	Place/Title	Date From	Date To
Heading	WO95/3078/4		
Heading	62nd Divl Mobile Vety Secn Jan 1917-1919 Aug		
War Diary	Northampton	10/01/1917	10/01/1917
War Diary	Southampton	11/01/1917	11/01/1917
War Diary	In The Field	12/01/1917	21/01/1917
War Diary	Frohen	22/01/1917	27/01/1917
War Diary	Bus	27/01/1917	19/02/1917
War Diary	Forceville	20/02/1917	23/03/1917
War Diary	Hamel	23/03/1917	11/04/1917
War Diary	Acheit Le Grand	12/04/1917	16/04/1917
War Diary	Acheit Le Grand	19/04/1917	31/05/1917
Heading	War Diary of 2/1st Mob. Vet. Section From 1st June 17 To 30th June 17 Volume VI		
War Diary	Achiet-Le-Grand	01/06/1917	14/06/1917
War Diary	Aduit-Le-Field	15/06/1917	16/06/1917
War Diary	Achiet Le Petit	17/06/1917	29/06/1917
War Diary	Favreuil	30/06/1917	30/06/1917
Heading	War Diary of 2/1st (W.R.) Mob. Vet. Section From 1st July To 31st July 1917 Vol VII		
War Diary	Favreuil	01/07/1917	31/07/1917
Heading	War Diary Of 2/1st (W.R.) Mobile Veterinary Section 1st Aug 1917 31st Aug 1917 Vol VIII		
War Diary	Favreuil	01/08/1917	31/08/1917
Heading	War Diary of 2/1st (W.R.) Mobile Veterinary Sector From Sept 1st 1917 To Sept 30th 1917 Volume IX		
War Diary	Favreuil	01/09/1917	30/09/1917
Heading	War Diary of 2/1st (WR) Mobile Veterinary Section From October 1st 1917 To October 31st 1917. Volume X		
War Diary	Favreuil	01/10/1917	11/10/1917
War Diary	Mesnil	12/10/1917	31/10/1917
War Diary	War Diary of 2/1st (WR) Mobile Veterinary Section From November 1st/17 To November 30th/17. Volume XI.		
War Diary	Monchiet	01/11/1917	13/11/1917
War Diary	Achiet-Le-Petit	14/11/1917	14/11/1917
War Diary	Barastre 174 C Central	15/11/1917	30/11/1917
Heading	War Diary Of 2/1 (W.R.) Mobile Veterinary Section. For December 1917		
War Diary	Bapaune	01/12/1917	04/12/1917
War Diary	Bailleulmont	05/12/1917	06/12/1917
War Diary	Freimcapelle	07/12/1917	14/12/1917
War Diary	Labeuvriere	15/12/1917	31/12/1917
Heading	War Diary Of 2/1 West Riding Mobile Veterinary Section 1st Jan 1918 To 31st Jan 1918 Vol XIII		
War Diary	Tinques	01/01/1918	08/01/1918
War Diary	Anzin	09/01/1918	31/01/1918
Heading	War Diary Of 2/1st (W.R.) Mobile Veterinary Section 1st February 1918 28th February 1918 Volume XIV		
War Diary	Anzin	01/02/1918	11/02/1918

War Diary	Vandelicourt	12/02/1918	28/02/1918
Heading	War Diary of 2/1 (WR) M.V.S. From 1-3-18 To 31-3-18 OC 2/1 WR MVS D.R. Crabb Capt A.V.C Vol XV		
War Diary	Vandelicourt	01/03/1918	03/03/1918
War Diary	Ecurie	04/03/1918	24/03/1918
War Diary	Berneville	25/03/1918	30/03/1918
War Diary	Thievres	31/03/1918	31/03/1918
Heading	War Diary Of 2/1st West Riding Mobile Veterinary Section 1st April 1918 To 30th April 1918 Volume 16		
War Diary	Thievres	01/04/1918	03/04/1918
War Diary	Pas en Artois	04/04/1918	07/04/1918
War Diary	Souastre	08/04/1918	08/04/1918
War Diary	Henu	09/04/1918	17/04/1918
War Diary	Pas-En-Artois	18/04/1918	31/05/1918
Heading	War Diary of 2/1st West Riding Mobile Veterinary Services From 1st June To 30th June 1918 Volume XVIII		
War Diary	Pas en Artois	01/06/1918	30/06/1918
Heading	War Diary of 2/1st (West Riding) Mobile Veterinary Section From 1st July 1918 To 31st July 1918 Volume 19		
War Diary	Pas en Artois	01/07/1918	15/07/1918
War Diary	Mailly	16/07/1918	17/07/1918
War Diary	Ecurie	18/07/1918	18/07/1918
War Diary	Tour	19/07/1918	20/07/1918
War Diary	Germain	21/07/1918	31/07/1918
Heading	War Diary of 2/1st W R Mobile Veterinary Section Volume XX From 1st August 1918 To 31st August 1918		
War Diary	Germaine	01/08/1918	01/08/1918
War Diary	Bisseuil	02/08/1918	03/08/1918
War Diary	Vertus	04/08/1918	04/08/1918
War Diary	Candas	05/08/1918	05/08/1918
War Diary	Sarton	06/08/1918	18/08/1918
War Diary	Saulty	19/08/1918	21/08/1918
War Diary	Sarton	22/08/1918	22/08/1918
War Diary	Saulty	23/08/1918	23/08/1918
War Diary	Bienvillers	24/08/1918	30/08/1918
War Diary	Douchy Les Ayette	31/08/1918	31/08/1918
Heading	War Diary of 2/1st W.R. Mobile Veterinary Section Volume XX From 1st August 1918 To 31st August 1918		
Heading	War Diary Of 2/1st (W.R.) Mobile Veterinary Section 1st Sept 1918 30th Sept 1918 Volume XXI		
War Diary	Douchy Les Ayette	01/09/1918	03/09/1918
War Diary	Gommiecourt	04/09/1918	10/09/1918
War Diary	Fremicourt	11/09/1918	25/09/1918
War Diary	Bertincourt	26/09/1918	28/09/1918
War Diary	Hermies	29/09/1918	30/09/1918
Heading	War Diary Of 2/1st W.R. Mob Veterinary Sec 1st Oct1918 To Oct 31st 1918 Volume XXII		
Miscellaneous	Cover For Documents. Nature Of Enclosures.		
War Diary	Hermies	01/10/1918	08/10/1918
War Diary	Haurincourt	09/10/1918	09/10/1918
War Diary	Masnieres	10/10/1918	10/10/1918
War Diary	Seranvillers	11/10/1918	13/10/1918

War Diary	Cattenieres	14/10/1918	15/10/1918
War Diary	Fresnoy Farm	16/10/1918	30/10/1918
War Diary	Tertre-Farm Fontaine	31/10/1918	31/10/1918
Heading	War Diary Of 2/1st (WR) Mobile Veterinary Section Nov 1st 1918 To Nov 30th 1918 Volume XXIII		
Miscellaneous	Cover For Documents. Nature Of Enclosures.		
War Diary	Tertre Farm	01/11/1918	03/11/1918
War Diary	Romires	04/11/1918	06/11/1918
War Diary	Oreinval	07/11/1918	08/11/1918
War Diary	Gommegnies	09/11/1916	09/11/1916
War Diary	Bavarian	10/11/1918	11/11/1918
War Diary	Bavarian	12/11/1918	18/11/1918
War Diary	Rousies	19/11/1918	19/11/1918
War Diary	Solre-Sur-Sambre	20/11/1918	24/11/1918
War Diary	Sarciernne	25/11/1918	25/11/1918
War Diary	Maradret Soroye	26/11/1918	27/11/1918
War Diary	Thynes	28/11/1918	30/11/1918
Heading	War Diary Of 2/1st (W R) Mobile Veterinary Section 1st Dec 1918 To 31st Dec 1918 Volume 24		
War Diary	Thynes	01/12/1918	10/12/1918
War Diary	Leignon	11/12/1918	11/12/1918
War Diary	Porcheresse	12/12/1918	12/12/1918
War Diary	Clavier	13/12/1918	13/12/1918
War Diary	Ville	14/12/1918	14/12/1918
War Diary	Rahier	15/12/1918	16/12/1918
War Diary	Petit Coo	17/12/1918	17/12/1918
War Diary	Weismes	18/12/1918	20/12/1918
War Diary	Elsenborn	21/12/1918	21/12/1918
War Diary	Kalter Herberg	22/12/1918	22/12/1918
War Diary	Herhahn	23/12/1918	24/12/1918
War Diary	Kaldenich	25/12/1918	31/12/1918
Heading	War Diary Of 2/1st W.R Mobile Veterinary Section 1st Jan 1919 To 31st Jan 1919 Volume 25		
Miscellaneous	Cover For Documents. Nature Of Enclosures.		
War Diary	Keldenich Germany	01/01/1919	31/01/1919
Heading	War Diary Of 2/1st (W.R.) Mobile Vet Sect 1st Feb 1919 To 28th Feb 1919 Volume 26		
War Diary	Keldenich Germany	01/02/1919	28/02/1919
War Diary	War Diary Of 2/1 (W.R.) Mobile Veterinary Section For March 1919 Volume III No III		
War Diary	Keldenich	01/03/1919	31/03/1919
Heading	War Diary of 2/1st (WR) Mobile Veterinary Section From 1st May 1919 To 31st May 1919		
War Diary	Soller	01/05/1919	31/05/1919
Heading	War Diary Of 2/1 (W.R.) Mobile Vety Section From 1.6.19 To 30.6.19 Volume XXX		
War Diary	Soller	01/06/1919	28/06/1919
Heading	War Diary of 2/1 (W.R.) Mobile Vety Section From 1.07.19 To 31.7.19		
War Diary	Soller Germany	01/07/1919	31/07/1919
Heading	War Diary Of 2/1 (W.R.) Mobile Vety Section Highland Division From 1.8.19 To 30.8.19		
War Diary	Soller Germany	01/08/1919	11/08/1919
War Diary	Blipstone Notts	12/08/1919	30/08/1919

WO95/30781/34

62ND DIVISION

~~2/1~~ WEST RIDING MOBILE VET SECN

62ND DIVL MOBILE VETY SECN.

JAN 1917 - ~~DEC 1918~~

1919 AUG

Original

Army Form C. 2118.

WAR DIARY
or
INTELLIGENCE SUMMARY.
(Erase heading not required.)

62nd Bde. Mobile Vety Section

Vol I

Place	Date	Hour	Summary of Events and Information	Remarks and references to Appendices
Northampton	Jan 10th 17	0500	Entrained for Southampton. 1 Officer (Capt. P. Alver A.V.C.) 27 Other Ranks. 26 Horses, 3 Vehicles.	
Southampton	11/7	1830	Embarked on S.S. "Manchester Importer" North Quay, anchored outside Le Havre 3 hours, went to become ringt. Landed disembarkation 1600 12/7. Locomotion.	
Anthrefield	12/7		Moved to Rest Rest Camp 103 at 2400 slept under Canvas.	
	13/7		Entrained to 6 Halles, left 1500, refreshments at Bonche & Abbeville.	
	14/7		Arrived thereat 1200, marched to station to Grand, 1800, billets, billets (fairly good) on horse lines en route which eventually recovered.	
	15/7		General Routine.	
	16/7		2 Sgts 2 L/Cpls 3 men offects. with section (6 head 6 9th LH Field Ambulance at Villers Bretonneux 2.)	
	17/7		Interview with O.D.V.S. 5th Army, received instructions.	
	18/7		Inspection of the Stationts. to defective.	
	19/7		Inspection of Horses in Sick lines by G.O.V.S. for evacuation. 2 aces pneumonia.	
	20/7		Evacuation of 30 Animals to B.V.H. Abbeville. 9 cpl in charge of Master Corporal Solon. (Oz Grand)	
	21/7			P. Alver Capt A.V.C. O.C. 62 Bde. M.V.S.

T.J.134. W.t. W708–770. 50000. 4/15. Sir J.C. & S.

Army Form C. 2118.

Original

WAR DIARY (2)
or
INTELLIGENCE SUMMARY.
(Erase heading not required.)

6 Divn Mobile Vety Section

Instructions regarding War Diaries and Intelligence Summaries are contained in F. S. Regs., Part II. and the Staff Manual respectively. Title pages will be prepared in manuscript.

Place	Date	Hour	Summary of Events and Information	Remarks and references to Appendices
Arthur	22/7		Motor broke with Div HQ 6" Beauvillers, billeted at 79 & Table d'Ore, billets poor. Picked up horse to by 525 Bty R.F.A. Large wound on top. No incident of importance happened.	
	23/7		Our supply wagon had to be brought in at night. Sent to Beco via Louvencourt. Arrived Beco 4pm, billets not allotted, stables at PNGs at Arthin Road, very poor. No casualties. Retired at 10.30 pm, up for general writing, Returned 4pm. Water supply proper. Paid 25 MCOS from 100 rgnt	
	24/7		"	
	25/7		"	
	26/7		4 Horses sent in to Hospital from 62" DAC. Retired 2am. Returned 7am.	
	27/7		"	
Beco	28/7		Moved to M.V. Camp of 49 and Div. Plus Lut thirds took over 1 horse 1 mule for M.V.S. of 49 and Div. Dick moved to Berteaucourt. General routine, had to go 2 miles to water due to front. 1 horse taken in from 486 Bty Reserve of water also 1 B 311" Byde, F 311" 2 B 311" R.F.A. & Hg Ars 311" (8 other carin)	
	29/7		General routine. 100% in 1 horses 312" Byde R.F.A. (Vaus) 1 9/5 Hfy R.A. pistol wound 3pm C Bty 312" R.F.A	

P Ahmcrofft Capt
OC 6 Divn Mobile N.V.C

Original

WAR DIARY
or
INTELLIGENCE SUMMARY.
(Erase heading not required.)

12 W Fus Mobile Vety Sectn

Army Form C. 2118.

Place	Date	Hour	Summary of Events and Information	Remarks and references to Appendices
Bav.	30/7		General Routine. 1 Horse taken in from S25 Coy A.S.C. 2 dogs taken along a.w.o.l. Major Taylor went to Hospital. 1 Horse taken away by 42nd M.F. Arranged for 2 Linesto for evacuating to B.V.H. only lot horses available	
"	31/7		16 Animals evacuated to No 22 V.H. Abbeville (12 Horses). Arranged for attendce to Several inspected Lieut Newman's charges, ordered destruction for Epstic Pneumonia	
"	1/8		Interviews with L.D.V.S. J. Comp about H.S.B.	

P. Abraye Capn AVC
O.C. 62nd Fus Mobile Vety Sectn

Original

VOLUME I WAR DIARY (4)
or
INTELLIGENCE SUMMARY. 62nd = No. Mobile Veterinary Section

Army Form C. 2118.

Place	Date	Hour	Summary of Events and Information	Remarks and references to Appendices
Duis	1 2/7		General Routine in Section & ADVS Office & NZA horses	Vol 2
"	2 6/7		Visited 312th Bde R.F.A. re mange also D.A.C. 62nd Divr. 16 animals evacuated to 6 B.V.H. (12 mange, 4 injuries)	
"	3 6/7		Sent half taken with animals sent to Athenville (N Vety Hospital) for feed	
"	4 7/7		Visited MDS 4th Div also inspected horses + 42 MVS Pertrecourt	
"	5 7/7		ADVS 5th Army inspected mange cases in MVS. Traine in 312 Bde R.F.A. Lemencourt	
"	6 7/7		Moved from Pertrecourt to Mametz lanes in MVS section	
"	6 6/7		Visited 310th Bde R.F.A. inspecting all horses evacuation satisfactory	
"	7 6/7		OA.S. Pertrecourt - Deleme RP inspecting all animals	
"	8		Inspecting 15 Reserve of War Camp horses over ruled to 798th Field (new ADS)	
"	9		Visit 46th Hy 15 Prisoner of War Camps T line Labour Battalion General horses	
"	10		" AV Signals R.E, 101 Hy Bde, R.A.H.Q. 11th Labour Field	
"	11		" Proceeded to Ingrepoindre ALS. the horses of the labour went morphine " Inspection of all horses in Later relieving cases for evacuation A.D.V. train & Delle: but RR Hd Qr, Div MOR AV Signals 188th Bty. Byrne.	
"	12		Evacuated 40 mange cases to Athenville, inspected by ADVS. Relieved	

Army Form C. 2118.

WAR DIARY
or
INTELLIGENCE SUMMARY.
(Erase heading not required.)

62nd Div: Motor Amb: Conv: Section

Place	Date	Hour	Summary of Events and Information	Remarks and references to Appendices
Bus	13/7		Sent 20 R Field Amb 186 Inf. Bde. Received 24 arrivals at 6. M.T.	
"	14/7		Returned 24 arrivals to M.T. Evacuated 40 arrivals to Hospital. (32 cases of mange) Sent 186 Inf Bde. to 2/2 W.R. Field Amb. (Return to 81 + 76 vacated)	
"	15/7		Sent RA arrivals + two MG Gps. inspecting all arrivals in M.T. arranged to take over 5 arrivals of 52nd arrivals for inspection.	
"	16		Evacuated 244 arrivals 6 to 22 B.V.H. Abbeville	
"	17		Sent RA + two MG Branches inspecting arrivals.	
"	18		General notice of M.T. Inspection of arrivals in M.T. for evacuation	
"	19		Evacuated of 29 arrivals at Beauval for 22 B.V.H. Abbeville including 8 mange cases	
Doxeville	20		Rented M.T. Lines at Bus. Sent no cases at Doxeville	
"	21		Sent 326, 327, 328 Coys. 62nd Div Siewn at Longvilliers	
"	22		" " several inspections of M.T.	
"	23		With C.O.T.L. moved lines at night. Passing of M.T.	
"	24		" " also sent 6 A.O.T. Bus	

August.

Army Form C. 2118.

WAR DIARY (6)
or
INTELLIGENCE SUMMARY. 62nd Divnl Mobile Vety Section

(Erase heading not required.)

Instructions regarding War Diaries and Intelligence Summaries are contained in F. S. Regs., Part II. and the Staff Manual respectively. Title pages will be prepared in manuscript.

Place	Date	Hour	Summary of Events and Information	Remarks and references to Appendices
Acheville	25/8/17		Visit to 62nd Divn. Train inspecting Carry Horses. General Routine M.V.S.	
	26/8/17		" at night	
			186th Infy Bde. Evacuated at Beaumont 38 Horses & 2 mules to 22 B.V.H.	
	27		62 Divn Train also at night, Inspection of MVS by ADVS.	
	28		" Evacuated from M.V.S. 14 animals	
			P. Oliver Capt. AVC OC 62nd Divn M.V.S.	

Army Form C. 2118.

WAR DIARY
or
INTELLIGENCE SUMMARY.
(Erase heading not required.)

Of A.R. Moore Fd. Sector

Vol 3

Place	Date	Hour	Summary of Events and Information	Remarks and references to Appendices
Doullens	March 1917			
	1		Visit 62nd Divisl. Genl. Hospachy 186th & 188th Bty Bdes at Mondry	
"	2		" " Visit to Naval casualty 6th G. Yorks Regt at night	
"	3		Arrivals. Interviews with ADOS at Paris	
"	4		ADS inspecting tactic turns of M.R. General Routine of A.D.S.	
"	5		Visit 2/3 WR Field Amb. 187th Hvy Arty Bde. "	
"	6		Evacuated 27 animals to No 22 Vety Hospital "	
"	7		Inspection of A.D.S. by A.D.V.S. "	
"	8		Evacuated twentyfour animals; Sergt Black sick sent to No 2 Vety Hospital Etaples	
"	9		Routine M.V.S.	
"	10		Visit 2/3 WR Field Amb. General Routine M.V.S.	
"	11		Evacuated 32 animals including one cart horse 1st 4th & 5th Corps	
"	12		Visit 92nd & 34th Machine Gun Corps. General Routine of M.V.S.	
"	13		Visit of A.D.V.S. General Routine of M.V.S.	
"	14		Evacuated 48 animals, including scores of lameness, General Routine of Lectures	
"	15		Visit 32nd Machine Gun sector. Visit of A.D.V.S. Paid men of M.V.S. Re Public and promo lectr	
"	16		Visit to A.D.S. Evacuated 16 animals 15 to 22 Vety Hospital (Étaples)	

Refual

Army Form C. 2118.

WAR DIARY
or
INTELLIGENCE SUMMARY.
(Erase heading not required.)

62 Qnd Divisional Mobile Veterinary Section

Instructions regarding War Diaries and Intelligence Summaries are contained in F. S. Regs., Part II. and the Staff Manual respectively. Title pages will be prepared in manuscript.

Place	Date	Hour	Summary of Events and Information	Remarks and references to Appendices
Foreville	15/3/17		Visit 2/8 W.R. Field Ambulance. General Routine of M.V.S.	
"	16		Evacuated 2 animals to No 22 B.V.H. General Routine of M.V.S.	
"	17		Mallened Mobile Section Horses. General Routine of M.V.S. Visit 2/8 W.R. Field Amb.	
"	18		Visit 232 Machine Gun Corps Horses. do.	
"	19		Evacuated 38 animals to No 22 Hospital do.	
"	20		Visit 2/3rd W.R. Field Amb. do.	
"	21		Visit by A.D.V.S. Y.S.O.S. do.	
"	22		Evacuated 35 animals to No 22 D.V.H. do.	
"	23		Moved to Naves. Visit by A.D.V.S. do.	
Naves	24		Julignes do.	
"	25		General Routine M.V.S.	
"	26		do. do. do. do. Visit 29 Toy A.S.C.	
"	27		do. do. do. do. 2/1 W.R. Field Amb.	
"	28		Evacuated 40 animals to No 7 B.V.S. Steps to cure Scabies of Scalor	
"	29		Visit Beaumont-Hamel. Evacuated 13 animals per 311 Field R.F.A.	
"	30		Paid men of M.V.S. General Routine M.V.S.	

T./134. Wt. W708–776. 50C0000. 4/15. Sir J. C. & S.

Army Form C. 2118.

WAR DIARY
or
INTELLIGENCE SUMMARY.
(Erase heading not required.)

Place	Date	Hour	Summary of Events and Information	Remarks and references to Appendices
Nauroz	31/3/7		Evacuated 93 wounds from 7 B.K.A. Several Review of Labour. P. Ahun Capt Ar.le. O.C. 241 W.R. Mobile Vety. Sectr.	

Army Form C. 2118.

WAR DIARY
or
INTELLIGENCE SUMMARY.
(Erase heading not required.)

Original

8/1 (OTC) Mobile Veterinary Section

Vol 4

Place	Date	Hour	Summary of Events and Information	Remarks and references to Appendices
Nauel	1/7/17		General Routine & evacuation of 93 animals to Hayes le came	
"	2		General Routine of Section. Erysipelatous are transferred to No 2 Vety. Hospital	
"	3		General Routine	
"	4		Visit to Miramont re movement of Section. General Routine	
"	5		General Routine	
"	6		"	
"	7		Move to Miramont to premises nr Station. General fatigues; evacuation of 95 animals	
"	8		General Routine	
"	9		"	
"	10		Evacuation of 68 animals to No 7 Vety Hospital	
"	11		Move to Achiet le Grand. Train by ADVS	
Achiet le Grand	12		General Routine	
"	13		Evacuates 64 animals to No 7 Veterinary Hospital train by ADVS	
"	14		General Routine	
"	15		"	
"	16		Evacuates 60 animals to No 7 Veterinary Hospital	

Army Form C. 2118.

WAR DIARY
or
INTELLIGENCE SUMMARY.
(Erase heading not required.)

Instructions regarding War Diaries and Intelligence Summaries are contained in F.S. Regs., Part II. and the Staff Manual respectively. Title pages will be prepared in manuscript.

Army No. 24(67) Mobile Vety Section

Place	Date	Hour	Summary of Events and Information	Remarks and references to Appendices
Alexandria	1917 June 18		General Routine. Visit by ADVS	
"	19		do do	Visit to 9th W.R. Field Amb.
"	20		do do	" 3rd Auxiliary Stamford Horses
"	21		do do	do Evacuated 112 animals to No 7 Veterinary Hospital
"	22		" "	do
"	23		" "	do
"	24		" "	do Visit to No 7 Veterinary Hospital
"	24		Evacuation of 93 animals to No 7 Veterinary Hospital	Visit to Bde Vet Gro animals
"	25		General Routine	do
"	26		General Routine. Hallowed 1 Sudan Horse, 8 HD. Horses + 12 WD. R.A.	
"	27		Evacuation of 12 animals to No) Veterinary Hospital. General Routine	
"	28		General Routine. Visit by ADVS.	
"	29		General Routine	do
"	30		do do	Conference with D.D.V.I. Army re Corps Mob. Vety Sect.
"	31		do do	Evacuation of 38 animals. Visit Bovelino [Codron]

P. Aben Capt AVC

Original

2/1st N.Z.M.R. Mobile Veterinary Section

WAR DIARY
or
INTELLIGENCE SUMMARY.
(Erase heading, not required.)

Instructions regarding War Diaries and Intelligence Summaries are contained in F.S. Regs., Part II. and the Staff Manual respectively. Title pages will be prepared in manuscript.

Place	Date	Hour	Summary of Events and Information	Remarks and references to Appendices
Asheik bag Ground	1-5-17		General Routine of Section; took duty charge of 161st Arty Bde (Capt Penn sick on leave); Evacuated sick to A.V.D.S. Evacuated 38 animals to Ayun Kara	
"	2-5-17		Visited by the A.D.V.S. General Routine of Section. Visited R.A.T. & Div H.Q. Br. arrived.	
"	3-5-17		Visited by A.D.V.S. General Routine of Section. Visited R.A.T. Div H.Q. Br. Evacuated	
"	4-5-17		General Routine. Evacuated 16 animals to Ayun Kara cause. Visited by A.D.V.S. Visited R.A.T. & Div H.Q. Br.	
"	5-5-17		General Routine. Visited by A.D.V.S. Visited R.A.T. Div H.Q. Br.	
"	6-5-17		"	
"	7-5-17		" Evacuated 17 animals to Ayun Kara cause	
"	8-5-17		Visited by A.D.V.S. Horses ex Helewah demonstration; 2 Return from Cav. ward 2/7 L.H.Fd. R.A.T. Div H.Q. Br.	
"	9-5-17		Evolution with A.D.V.S. Demonstration of Horses ex Helewah there 7/WR Field Ambulance. Visited R.A.T. Div H.Q. Br.	
"	10-5-17		by A.D.V.S. Change Commencement; Visited R.A.T. Div H.Q. Div Br. Horses	

WAR DIARY
or
INTELLIGENCE SUMMARY

Army Form C. 2118.

(Erase heading not required.)

2/1 WR Mobile Vety Section

Place	Date	Hour	Summary of Events and Information	Remarks and references to Appendices
Achiet le Grand	11-5-17		General Routine. Evacuated 16 animals to Forges les Eaux. Visit Behencourt R.A. & Divl. H.Q. Dr. Visited by A.D.V.S.	
	12-5-17		General Routine. Attached men returned to their units. Visited Army Workshop.	
			A.D.V.S. Visited R.A. & Divl. H.Q. Dr.	
	13-5-17		General Routine. Visited by A.D.V.S.	
	14-5-17		Visit of Major W[?] Littledales Divl. 186th Inf. Bde with A.D.V.S. General Routine.	
	15-5-17		General Hare & Major Serran inspected Mobile Vety Section. Evacuated 20 animals to Forges les Eaux (Seven Strays). General working of Section.	
	16-5-17		General Routine. Visited by A.D.V.S. Visited Brig. & R.A. H.Q. 62 animals	
	17-5-17		"	
	18-5-17		General Routine. Evacuated 5 animals to Forges les Eaux. Visited by A.D.V.S.	
			Visited R.A. & Divl. H.Q. 60 animals	
	19-5-17		General Routine. A.D.V.S. Divl. Vety. Walker out always with cutting telephone wire. Contains Lovely representatives. Visited S.A.P.O.S. re Anti-working flags. Armored duties of A.D.V.S. Major Hall leaving for on leave. Visited 316th Bde R.F.A.	
			3 animals reared to be sent to M.V.S.	

MOBILE VET SUMMARY
SECTION 20.5.17
No. MV/832
Date.........

T2134. Wt. W708-776. 50C000. 4/15. Sir J.C. & S.

WAR DIARY

Army Form C. 2118.

Instructions regarding War Diaries and Intelligence Summaries are contained in F. S. Regs., Part II. and the Staff Manual respectively. Title pages will be prepared in manuscript.

WAR DIARY or INTELLIGENCE SUMMARY.
(Erase heading not required.)

2/1st W.R. Mobile Vety Section

April 1917

Place	Date	Hour	Summary of Events and Information	Remarks and references to Appendices
(continued)				
Rouen	21.5.17		Visited HQ, Div. & R.A. Horses. Visited 2/1st & 2/3rd (W.R.) Field Ambs.; 186th Infantry Bde.	
Le Brand			& 2/3rd Machine Gun Corps. General routine of section.	
"	22.5.17		Visited Reformery, inspected arrival of Remounts. Visited R.A.T. Div. & Coy.	
			Inspected arrival of sick Railway troops injured by accident.	
"	23.5.17		Visited 3/12th Bde R.A. & Bde. instructed send 6 animals to M.V.S.	
			Visited 2/2 (W.R.) Field Amb. (animals much improved). Visited 2/8th West Yorks.	
			206th Machine Gun Corps. Hd. Qr. Div. T.R.A. animals. S.O.6s horse picked up	
			rail. Visited 5.28 Bty R.G.A. Received 2 LD mules & complete 6 stab of M.V.S.	
"	24.5.17		Visited 201 Machine Gun Corps.; 460 Coy R.E.; 2/5 & 2/L Reg.l.; 24 R.O.4.2.9 Reg.l. 2/4	
			V.T.L. Reg.l.; 461 & Coy R.E.; 457 Coy R.E. I S.O.6s horse returned with eye	
			lost re 310th Bde R.F.A.	
"	25.5.17		Visited 310th Bde R.F.A. Visited Div. T.R.A. Hd Qr. Animals. Evacuated 13 animals	
			to troops - Ex sinnes (Steam of 62 Division). Interview F.O.S. re F2000	
			General routine of section.	
	26.5.17		Visited 62nd D.F.C. No 2 section in good condition. to No.1 Vee Infirmary. Visited	
			Div. T.R.A. Hd. Qrs. Relieved at 2ots mare. Examined remounts from Home Lg?	

2/1st (W.R.) MOBILE VETERINARY SECTION.
No. MV/867.

Original

2/1st K.F. Mobile Vety Section. Army Form C. 2118.
62nd Division

WAR DIARY
or
INTELLIGENCE SUMMARY.
(Erase heading not required.)

Place	Date	Hour	Summary of Events and Information	Remarks and references to Appendices
Continued				
Achiet-le-Grand	26-5-17		Meet Jg of Sin van Horse (Inspection). R.I.O's mule injured by shrapnel & taken into M.V.S.	
Grevis	27-5-17		Visited 62nd Div Signals animals. R.A. & Div. H.Q. Grs. Visited No 1 section 62nd M.C. General Routine of M.V.S.	
"	28-5-17		Visited 312th Bde R.F.A. (Certificate of animals inspected). 3 animals ordered to M.V.S. Visited 62nd Div Signal Co. Visited R.A.T. Div. H.Q. Grs. Visited Railway troops.	
"	29-5-17		Visited 527, 526 & 528 Coys A.S.C. Visited 10/1 Div H.Q. Grs. Coys laundries. Visited total stables re allotment of animals for duty. 5 remounts 13 animals.	
"	30-5-17		16 Forge-les-eaux (6 mange) 12 animals of 62 Division General Routine of M.V.S. Visited R.A. & Div H.Q. Grs. Visited accident cases at Advist Station. Animal brought into M.V.S. Examined 2 consignees for animals of Div. H.Q. Grs. General Routine of M.V.S.	
"	31-5-17		Visited 312th Bde R.F.A. (all animals improved) Visited 525 Coy A.S.C. Visited R.A. & Div. H.Q. Grs.	

P. Olden Capt A.V.C.
O.C. 2/1st (W.R.) Mobile Veterinary Section.

2/1st (W.R.)
MOBILE VETERINARY
SECTION.
No.............
Date.............

Original

Confidential Vol 6

War Diary
of
Mob. Vet. Section
2/Mob

From 1st June 17. to 30th June 17.

Volume VI

Original

Army Form C. 2118.

WAR DIARY
or
INTELLIGENCE SUMMARY.
(Erase heading not required.)

Army Form C. 2118. 2/1st W.R. Mobile Veterinary Section
B. Brownson

No. MV/1086.
Date 2/7/17.
MOBILE VETERINARY SECTION

Place	Date	Hour	Summary of Events and Information	Remarks and references to Appendices
Achiet le	1-6-17		Evac'd R.A. + Div. H'd Qr animals. M.M.P. Evacuated 2 aeroplanes of same. Evacuated 6 aeroplanes out by Capt. Mark. R.V.C. (One positive Farcy+). Evacuated 4 animals to Corps Cas. Same. Major Hall A.V.S. returned from leave and took over to turn.	
Mens	2-6-17		General routine of Section. Visited by A.D.V.S.	
"	3-6-17		Evac'd R.A. + Div. H'd Qrs. Evacuated aeroplane to W.B. Horse as 27 (Equine). Visited by A.D.V.S. General routine of Section. Evac'd M.M.P. animals.	
"	4-6-17		Evac'd R.A. + Div. H'd Qrs. + M.M.P. Evacuated 186th Infantry Brigade of casuals. Le Petit. Visited by A.D.V.S. General routine of Section.	
"	5-6-17		Took over veterinary charge of 186th Infantry Brigade. Drew Funk Rail-way Inspn throw. Evac'd 186th Infy Bde. (Operator on foot 24 miles of Wellington Regt). Evac'd R.A. + Div. H'd Qr animals. Visited by A.D.V.S. Evacuated 8 animals (16 of 62 Evac'd.) Evac'd R.A. + Div H'd Qr animals.	
"	6-6-17		Visited M.M.P. animals. Evacuated aeroplane. Evac'd R.A. + Div. H'd Qr animals; 186th Infy Bde.; visited by A.D.V.S. General Routine of Section.	
"	7-6-17		Evac'd R.A. + Div. H'd Qr animals. M.M.P. Lost aeroplane (Mephisto hos 285, 269	

T2134. Wt. W708—776. 50000. 4/15. Sir J. C. & S.

Original

17

Army Form C. 2118.

WAR DIARY
or
INTELLIGENCE SUMMARY.

(Erase heading not required.)

Instructions regarding War Diaries and Intelligence Summaries are contained in F.S. Regs., Part II. and the Staff Manual respectively. Title pages will be prepared in manuscript.

D/ L.R. Mobile Veterinary Section
62nd Division

Place	Date	Hour	Summary of Events and Information	Remarks and references to Appendices
Achiele Grand.	7/6/17 (contd)		M.M.P. to 20. Bri Hd Qr ho 28. (all negative) General Routine of Section.	
"	8-6-19		Evacuated 13 animals (5 mange) 10 animals of 62nd Division (one horse shot) Visited Hd. Qr. RA & Division. Evacuated scrapings from D.A.C. (3 positive) General Routine of M.V.S.	
"	9-6-19		Evacuated scrapings from 313 & R.A. & 166th Arty Bde. General Routine of M.V.S. Proceeded on leave to England. Handed over command of M.V.S. to Capt Croft A.V.C	
"	10-6-19		Took command of 62nd Bn M.V.S. over from Capt P Clow A.V.C. Visited H.Q Division and H.Q R.A. Horses. Visited by A.D.V.S. General Routine of Section.	JRC
"	11-6-19		Visited H.Q Division and H.Q R.A. horses. Visited by A.D. V.S. General routine M.V.S.	DNL
"	12-6-19		Evacuated & animals 5 Circle mange all 62nd Division. General Routine of M.V.R. Visited by A.D.V.S. Visited H.Q Division horses. Evacuated scrapings from M.M.Phos Positive	DNL
"	13-6-19		Evac scrapings of 3 horses B/312 — negative results. Visited by A.D.V.S. General routine M.V.S.	JRC
"	14-6-19		General Routine of M.V.S. Visited H.Q Y.R.A. & Division. Visited by A.D.V.S.	JRC

Original

WAR DIARY or INTELLIGENCE SUMMARY

Army Form C. 2118.

No. R. Mobile Veterinary Section 2/1 of R Mobile Veterinary Section

(Erase heading not required.)

Place	Date	Hour	Summary of Events and Information	Remarks and references to Appendices
Achiet-le-Petit	15-6-17		Evacuated 11 animals 8 mange, 1 of 46 Reserve Park. General review of M.V.S. Camp Shelled	726
	16-6-17		No casualties. Visited by A.D.V.S.	690
	17-6-17		General Routine of M.V.S. Visited by A.D.V.S.	5728
Achiet-le-Petit	17-6-17		Shifted camp to Achiet-le-Petit. General routine of M.V.S. Visited by A.D.V.S.	5718
	18-6-17		Enlarged Isolation — inspection rounds. General routine. Visited by A.D.V.S.	
	19-6-17		Evacuated 7 animals all 63rd Division. Elementary Veterinary. General Routine of M.V.S.	9702
	20-6-17		Visited H.Q. Division. General Routine of M.V.S. Visited by A.D.V.S.	9708
	21-6-17		Visited H.Q. Division. General Routine of M.V.S. Visited by A.D.V.S.	D702
	22-6-17		Returned from leave took over duties from Capt. Croft C.O.S. General Routine of M.V.S.	
			Evacuated 6 animals to Hayes-les-baux (3 mange) Visited by A.D.V.S.	
	23-6-17		Visited Division H.Q. Gp. & 188th Infantry Bde. M.M.P.: Lectures inspected by	
			A.D.V.S. Corps & A.D.V.S. Division. General Routine of M.V.S.	
	24-6-17		Visited Div. H.Q. Gp. & M.M.P. Visited by A.D.V.S. General Routine of M.V.S.	
			Visited with A.D.V.S. new camp at Sacrament occupied by 20th Bn. Notts.	
	25-6-17		Visited H.Q. Gp. Div.; 188th Infy. Bde. M.M.P. Visited by A.D.V.S. General	
			Routine of M.V.S.	

"Original"

Army Form C. 2118.

2/1 (W.R.) Mobile Veterinary Section

WAR DIARY
or
INTELLIGENCE SUMMARY.
(Erase heading not required.)

Instructions regarding War Diaries and Intelligence Summaries are contained in F. S. Regs., Part II. and the Staff Manual respectively. Title pages will be prepared in manuscript.

Place	Date	Hour	Summary of Events and Information	Remarks and references to Appendices
Achiet le Petit	26-6-17		Visited Div. H.Q. Bn., M.M.P. & 15th Reserve Park A.S.C. Evacuated 3 animals to Forps-le-eaume. Visited Favreuil inspected new Camp. C.O. M.V.S. 25th Div. called to view. Visited by A.D.V.S. & M.O. General Routine of M.V.S.	
"	27-6-17		General Routine of M.V.S. Visited by A.D.V.S. Disarmed spark in the afternoon	
"	28-6-17		Visited Div. H.Q. Bn., 15th Reserve Park A.S.C., A.D.V.S. Office, 11th Labour Battn. Paid Re men of M.V.S. Visited by A.D.V.S. General Routine of M.V.S.	
"	29-6-17		Visited by A.D.V.S. General Routine of M.V.S. Section moved to Favreuil. Visited Div. H.Q. Bn., Allowed A.D.V.S. Office in evening the informed me that I had been made F.A.D.V.S. 51st Division	
Favreuil	30-6-17		General Routine of M.V.S. Visited H.S. Qrs. Division F.A.D.V.S	

P. Abson Capt. A.V.C.
O.C. 2/1 (W.R.) Mobile Vet Section

Original

Confidential

No 7

War Diary

of

2/1st (N.R.) Mot. Vet. Section.

From 1st July to 31st July 1917.

Vol VII

Army Form C. 2118.

WAR DIARY
or
INTELLIGENCE SUMMARY.
(Erase heading not required.)

2/1st W.R. Mobile Veterinary Section

Instructions regarding War Diaries and Intelligence Summaries are contained in F.S. Regs., Part II. and the Staff Manual respectively. Title pages will be prepared in manuscript.

Place	Date	Hour	Summary of Events and Information	Remarks and references to Appendices
Farewell	1-7-17		Handed over command of M.V.S. to Capt André A.V.C.	
"	1-7-17		Took over command of 2/1(W.R.) M.V.S. from Capt Alton A.V.C. being commanded to do so by A.D.V.S. 62nd Division. Visited by D.A.D.V.S. Visited D.H.Q. and Div. Train. General routine of Section. Complied with A.R.O. 1912 (2)	(PC) 1017 Capt A.
	2-7-17		General routine of Section. Visited D.H.Q. and Field Ambulances and Train. Visited by D.A.D.V.S.	
	3-7-17		Evacuated 6 animals, at taken over, from 52 M.V.S. Visited by D.A.D.V.S. and by D.D.V.S. 5th Corps. Visited D.H.Q. and Train. General routine of Section.	
	4-7-17		General routine of Section. Visited by D.A.D.V.S. Visited D.H.Q. Train. H.Q. R.A. and H.Q. R.E. horses. also Field Ambulances. Signal Coy.	
	5-7-17		General Routine of Section. Visited by D.A.D.V.S. Visited D.H.Q. and Train. Commenced to lay down Lock standings for horses in Section.	
	6-7-17		General Routine of M.V.S. Visited by D.A.D.V.S. Visited D.H.Q. and Train. also Field Ambulances.	

2/1st (W.R.) MOBILE VETERINARY SECTION.
No. MY/273.
Date 1/8/17.

T/134. Wt. W708—776. 50000. 4/15. Sir J. C. & S.

WAR DIARY
or
INTELLIGENCE SUMMARY

Army Form C. 2118.

2/1(W.R) M.V.S.

Place	Date	Hour	Summary of Events and Information	Remarks and references to Appendices
Fauvril	7-7-17		General Routine of M.V.S. Visited D.H.Q. and Signal Coy. Visited by D.A.D.V.S.	
	8-7-17		General routine of M.V.S. Visited 2/1 A.D.V.S. Visited D.A.Q. and Div Train	
	9-7-17		General routine of M.V.S. Visited by D.A.D.V.S. Visited Field Ambulances Signal Coy & H.Q. RA and H.Q. 62nd Division. No 7703273 Pte Tetley evacuated 14 days to 2 Field Punishment for alarm without cause	
	10-7-17		General Routine of section Visited D.A.Q. Divisional Train and H.Q. R.A. Visited by A.D.V.S.	
	11-7-17		General Routine of Section Visited D.H.Q. Visited by A.D.V.S.	
	12-7-17		General Routine of Section Visited 2/1 a.D.V.S. Visited D.T. Sent Coy train	
	13-7-17		General Routine of Section Visited G.a.D.V.S. No SE 2093 S.S. Outfield L/Cp reported from No 13 Base Very Hospital for duty. Evacuated 5 animals a/c of deficiencies	
	14-7-17		General Routine of Section Visited D.H.Q & Div Ambulances and Div Train.	
	15-7-17		General Routine of Section Visited by A.D.V.S. Visited D.H.Q & Div Train.	

2/1st (W.R.) MOBILE VETERINARY SECTION.

Original

WAR DIARY
INTELLIGENCE SUMMARY

Army Form C. 2118.

2/1st W.R. Mobile Veterinary Section.

Place	Date	Hour	Summary of Events and Information	Remarks and references to Appendices
Fureuil	16-7-17		General Routine of Section. Visited by D.A.D.V.S. Visited D.A.Q and Field Ambulances.	
	17-7-17		General Routine of Section, Evacuated 10 animals, 5 of 62 Div, 5 of 293 Brigade R.F.A. 2 horses of 62 Div, 2 horses of 293 Bde. Visited Horsemen.	
	18-7-17		General Routine of Section. Visited by D.A.D.V.S. Visited D.H.Q	
	19-7-17		General Routine of Section. Visited by D.A.D.V.S. Visited D.H.Q Aq R.E. & H.Q.R.A. and Field Ambulances also Div Train	21.7
	20-7-17		General Routine of Section. Evacuated 5 animals, all 62 Div.	23/7
	21-7-17		General Routine of Section. Visited D.H.Q, R.A. (R.E.) & Div Train	
	22-7-17		General Routine of Section. Visited by D.A.D.V.S. and visited D.H.Q & Div Train.	
	23-7-17		General Routine of Section. Visited by D.A.D.V.S. & visited D.H.Q. Also Field Ambulances.	
	24-7-17		General Routine of Section. Visited by D.A.D.V.S. & visited Div Train, Also D.H.Q, R.A. & R.E.	
	25-7-17		General Routine of Section. Visited by D.A.D.V.S. and visited D.H.Q & Div Train.	

2/1st (W.R.)
MOBILE VETERINARY
SECTION.
No. ....
Date 1/8/17

Army Form C. 2118.

WAR DIARY
or
INTELLIGENCE SUMMARY. 2/1 (2/R) Mobile Veterinary See E.F.R

(Erase heading not required.)

Place	Date	Hour	Summary of Events and Information	Remarks and references to Appendices
General	26-7-17		General Routine of Section. Visited by D.A.D.V.S. and visited 1/8.6th Bgd Sph Brigade & Capt Stroud Relde on leave.	
	27-7-17		General Routine of Section. Evacuated 14 animals all O2 Divisions	
	28-7-17		General Routine of Section. Visited by D.A.D.V.S. and visited Grain and Field Ambulances.	
	29-7-17		General Routine of Section. Visited D.H.Q and M.G R.A. and R.E. Also see Train.	
	30-7-17		General Routine of Section. Visited by D.A.D.V.S. and visited D.H.Q. Also Field Ambulances	
	31-7-17		General Routine of Section. Visited the Train along with D.A.D.V.S.	

2/1st (W.R.)
MOBILE VETERINARY
SECTION.
No. M/1273.
Date 1/8/17

Original   Vol 8

Confidential
War Diary
of
31st A.R. Mobile Veterinary Section

1st Aug 1917   31st Aug 1917

Vol. VIII

WAR DIARY
or
INTELLIGENCE SUMMARY.
(Erase heading not required.)

Army Form C.2118
No. M/149/
Date 2/9/17

Original

2/1 (WR) Mobile Veterinary Section

Place	Date	Hour	Summary of Events and Information	Remarks and references to Appendices
Jawenick	1-8-17		Visited D.H.Q. and Divisional Train, Ordinary Routine of Section. Visited D.A.D.V.S.	S.R.B.
	2-8-17		Visited Field Ambulances also Signal Coy and D.H.Q., Ordinary Routine of M.V.S. Visited 156th Infantry Bde.	S.R.B.
	3-8-17		Visited by D.A.D.V.S. Visited 15.6th Infantry Bde. Examined 14 animals (horses 10, mules 4) 11 of 62nd Division, 3 of 293 Brigade R.F.A. of superior range, 2 range mentals. (3 suspect mange cases from 62 Division) Visited LGOA D.V.S. and visited H.Q.R.E. & 119 R.A. Brigade.	S.R.B.
	4-8-17		Visited Divisional Train, D.H.Q. and Field Ambulances. Ordinary Routine of M.V.S.	S.R.B.
	5-8-17		Visited D.H.Q. Signal Coy and Divisional Train (52's Coy). Visited by D.A.D.V.S. Ordinary routine of M.V.S.	S.R.B.
	6-8-17		Visited D.H.Q. and Field Ambulances. Visited by D.A.D.V.S. and ordinary Routine of M.V.S.	S.R.B.
	7-8-17		Visited D.H.Q. and Divisional Train. Ordinary Routine of Section.	S.R.B.
	8-8-17		Staff Sergt Dutfield returned for duty on return from leave. Ordinary Routine of Section. Visited Divisional Train and H.Q R.E. and R.A. also Signal Coy.	S.R.B.

F. P. Cobb Capt. AVC (TF)

WAR DIARY
or
INTELLIGENCE SUMMARY.
(Erase heading not required.)

Army Form C. 2118.

2/1st (W.R.) Mob. Veterinary Section

Place	Date	Hour	Summary of Events and Information	Remarks and references to Appendices
Tournai	9-8-17		Ordinary routine of Section. Visited by A.D.V.S.	J.P.6
	10-8-17		Evacuated 2000 animals (horses & 2 mules) all 62nd Division. DAQ also full cases of mange. Visited Divisional train and DAQ also ambulances. Ordinary Routine of Section.	J.P.6
	11-8-17.		Visited Field Ambulances. D.H.Q. H.Q. R.E. and H.Q. R.A. also Signal Coy. Attacked elsewhere. Show of Horses. General Routine of Section.	J.P.6
	12-8-17		General Section Routine. Visited Div. Train and D.H.Q.	J.P.6
	13-8-17		General routine of Section. Visited D.H.Q. and Signal Coy. o 2/2 Rifle Ambulance	J.P.6
	14-8-17		General routine of Section. Visited D.H.Q. and Div. train. Visited 9 D.M.V.T.	J.P.6
	15-8-17		General routine of Section. Sgt. Walton proceeded to Havre & enlist for 1 Year. M.16 Inst. Visited D.H.Q., H.Q. R.E. and H.Q. R.A. of Division. Visited field ambulances 2/1 and 2/3rd. Visited 9 D.M.V.T.	J.P.6
	16-8-17		General routine of Section. Visited D.M.Q. and Div. Train.	J.P.6
	17-8-17		Evacuated twenty seven animals, eleven of them from 62 Division, seven mange cases four mange from 62 Division	J.P.6

D.T. Groves (F.)

2/1st (W.R.)
MOBILE VETERINARY
SECTION
Army Form C.2118.
No. MV/491
Date 1/9/17

WAR DIARY
or
INTELLIGENCE SUMMARY.
(Erase heading not required.)

2/1(WR) Mobile Veterinary Section

Instructions regarding War Diaries and Intelligence Summaries are contained in F. S. Regs., Part II. and the Staff Manual respectively. Title pages will be prepared in manuscript.

Place	Date	Hour	Summary of Events and Information	Remarks and references to Appendices
Louvrval	18-8-17		General Routine of Section. Visited Field Ambulances. H.Q. Div Train and D.H.Q. Visited by A.D.V.S. Visited Signal Coy.	JFB
	19-8-17		General routine of Section. Visited Divisional Train. Visited by D.A.D.V.S.	JFB
	20-8-17		General routine of Section. Visited D.H.Q and Field Ambulances 2/1 and 2/3	JFB
	21-8-17		Evacuated sixteen animals, one from the 62nd Divison Officer from #1 Divison. General routine of Section. Visited by D.A.D.V.S.	JFB
	22-8-17		General routine of Section. Visited D.H.Q. HQ RB & HQ RE. and Div Train.	JFB
	23-8-17		General routine of Section. Visited DHQ and Field Ambulances. Signal Coy.	JFB
	24-8-17		Evacuated Forty eight animals, one from 62 Div. and one from H Corps Hosp. and forty six from J.W.R Train. General routine of Section. Visited by D.A.D.V.S.	J.D.
	25-8-17		General Routine of Section. Visited D.H.Q. and Div Train. & 2/2 Field Ambulance.	JFB
	26-8-17		General Routine of Section. Visited Div Train 3 Corps and 2/1 & 2/3 Field Ambulances.	JFB
	27-8-17		General Routine of Section. Visited Div Train D.H.O. and HQ R.A. HQ R.B. Visited by A.D.V.S.	JFB
	28-8-17		Evacuated 15 animals none of them from 62 Divsn. Visited 3 Bde Coys J Train and D.H.Q also Signal Coy. J.R. Staff Capt and A.V.	JFB

T.2134. Wt. W708—776. 500000. 4/15. Sir J. C. & S.

2/1st (W.R.)
MOBILE VETERINARY
SECTION

Army Form C. 2118.
M/1441
39/9

Original

2/1 (WR) Mobile Veterinary Section

WAR DIARY
INTELLIGENCE SUMMARY
(Erase heading not required.)

Instructions regarding War Diaries and Intelligence Summaries are contained in F.S. Regs., Part II. and the Staff Manual respectively. Title pages will be prepared in manuscript.

Place	Date	Hour	Summary of Events and Information	Remarks and references to Appendices
Perenne	29-8-17		General Routine of Section. Visited 2 H.Q. & H.Q. R.A. also 2A.S.T.T.	TP8
	30-8-17		General Routine of Section. Visited Div Train 277-9.	TP6
	31-8-17		Evacuated eight animals, two from 62 Division Section unfested by 2.D.V.S. 3rd Army. General routine of Section. Visited D.A.Q. Field Ambulances.	TP6

J.R. Craft
Capt Corps W(T)

O.C. 2/ (WR) M V.T.

T2134. Wt. W708—776. 50000. 4/15. Sir J. C. & S.

ORIGINAL

Vol 9

Confidential
War Diary
of
2/1st (W.R.) Mobile Veterinary Section.

From Sept. 1st 1917.   To Sept. 30th 1917.

Volume IX.

WAR DIARY

INTELLIGENCE SUMMARY. 2/1 (W.R.) Mobile Veterinary Section

Army Form C. 2118.

MOBILE VETERINARY SECTION

Place	Date	Hour	Summary of Events and Information	Remarks and references to Appendices
Danvich	1-9-17		General routine of Section. Visited 62nd Divisional Train in company with D.D.V.S.	(J.R.E)
	2-9-17		General routine of Section. Visited D.H.Q, H.Q. R.E. & R.A and Signal Coy also 2/1 and 2/3 (W.R) Field Ambulances. No. 03282 Pte M?Hill returned 246.P.S. declared a.m.	(J.R.E.) (J.R.E)
	3-9-17		General routine of Section. Visited Divisional Train and D.H.Q.	
	4-9-17.		Evacuated 10 animals, three of them from 62nd Division. 2 cases of Mange one mange being from 62nd Division.	(J.R.E)
	5-9-17.		General routine of Section. Visited D.H.Q. 2/2(W.R) Field Ambulance also General Routine of Section.	(J.R.E)
	6-9-17.		General Routine. Section. Visited Sig? A.D.D. and visited Divisional Train	(J.R.E)
	7-9-17.		General Routine of Section. No S.E. 21962 Pt Riffe W.J returned to duty from 2/3 W.R Field Ambulance. Visited 2/1 & 2/3 Field Ambulances and D.H.Q	(J.R.E)
	8-9-17.		General routine of Section. Visited Divisional Train and D.H.Q also H.Q R.E & R.E. also Signals Coy	(J.R.E)
	9-9-17		General Routine of Section. Visited 3 Brigade Coy of Div Train, also D.M.S Signals Coy	(J.R.E)
	10-9-17		General Routine of Section. Pte Gyles No 77.03268 evacuated hospital with D.A.H F.R Crabbe	(J.R.E)

WAR DIARY

2/1 (W.R.) Mobile Veterinary Section

Form C. 2118.

INTELLIGENCE SUMMARY

(Erase heading not required.)

21st (W.R.) MOBILE VETERINARY SECTION
No. M/1652
Date: 11/9/17

Place	Date	Hour	Summary of Events and Information	Remarks and references to Appendices
Journée	11-9-17		Evacuated 15 animals eleven from 62nd Division. General review of Station. Visited Divisional Train and 2/2 Field Ambulance.	DRB
	12-9-17		General review of Section. Visited D.H.Q. and H.Q. R.A., H.Q. R.E. of 62nd Division. Visited 2/1 and 2/3 (W.R.) Field Ambulance.	DRB
	13-9-17		General review of Section. Visited D.A.D.V.S. and visit by D.A.D.V.S. Visited D.H.Q. and Divisional Train & Companies.	DRB
	14-9-17		General review of Section. Visited Signal Coy. and S.H.Q.	DRB
	15-9-17		Visited 2/2 (W.R.) Field Ambulance and Signal Coy, also D.H.Q. General Routine of Section.	DRB
	16-9-17		Took over duties of D.A.D.V.S. during absence of Major Kell on Tour. Visited 2/1 and 2/3 (W.R.) Field Ambulances also D.H.Q. and Signal Coy. General Routine of Section.	DRB
	17-9-17		Visited D.H.Q. and Divisional Train also 2/2 (W.R.) Field Ambulance. General routine of Section.	DRB
	18-9-17		Visited 3 Brigade Companies of Divisional Train, 2/1 Field Ambulance, D.H.Q. and H.Q. R.A. and R.E. Pte Bradley went on tour D.V.K. General routine of Section.	DRB
			Evacuated 9 animals, sick, three from 62nd Division.	
	19-9-17		Visited 2/2 Field Ambulance, 325 Coy A.S.C., Signal Coy and D.H.Q. General Routine of Section.	DRB

WAR DIARY 2/1 (WR) Mobile Veterinary Section Army Form C. 2118.

INTELLIGENCE SUMMARY.
(Erase heading not required.)

Original

2/1st (W.R.) MOBILE VETERINARY SECTION
No. M4/652
Date. 4/10/17

Place	Date	Hour	Summary of Events and Information	Remarks and references to Appendices
Farreuil	20-9-17		General routine of Section. Visited 3 Brigade Coys of Divisional Train also DHQ and 2/1 and 2/3 (WR) Field Ambulance.	See
	21-9-17		General routine of Section. Visited DHQ, Signal Coy and 625 by A.S.C.	See
	22-9-17		Attended Conference A.D.V.S. VI Corps. Visited D.H.Q. General routine of Section.	See
	23-9-17		General routine of Section. Visited Div Train and DHQ, also 2/1 and 2/3 Field Ambulances. Snow also while quartier.	See
	24-9-17		General routine of Section. Visited DHQ, Signal Coy and 525 by A.C.	See
	25-9-17		General routine of Section. Evacuees & animals, mare from 62 Division.	See
	26-9-17		Visited DHQ, Div Train and 2/1 (WR) Field Ambulance. General Railway Meeting.	See
	27-9-17		Visited 2/3 (WR) Field Ambulance, DHQ and Divisional Train. General routine of Section.	See
	28-9-17		Visited 2/2 Field Ambulance, Signal Coy and D.H.Q. General routine of Section.	See
	29-9-17		Visited No 1 Section SAC in consultation with Capt Brown AVC. Visited DHO on Company with Lt DAD.V.S. Visited Divisional Train, Lt Brierly returned from leave. General routine of Section.	See
	30-9-17		General Routine. Visited Visited DHQ and Divisional Train. J.R. Leath Capt AVC (V)	See

Confidential

War Diary

of

2/1st (W.R.) Mobile Veterinary Section.

From October 1st 1917   To   October 31st 1917.

Volume X.

Army Form C. 2118.

No. M/183
Date 2/11/19

2/1st (W.R.)
MOBILE VETERINARY
SECTION.

WAR DIARY
or
INTELLIGENCE SUMMARY. 2/1(WR) Mobile Veterinary Section

(Erase heading not required.)

Instructions regarding War Diaries and Intelligence Summaries are contained in F. S. Regs., Part II. and the Staff Manual respectively. Title pages will be prepared in manuscript.

Place	Date	Hour	Summary of Events and Information	Remarks and references to Appendices
Fauneuil	1-10-17		Visited 2/5 Duke of Wellingtons Rgt. D.H.Q, and Signal Company 62nd Div. Also visited 2/1 and 2/3 (WR) Field Ambulances, and 526, 527, and 528 Coys A.S.C. General routine of Section.	S.R.B.
	2-10-17		Visited D.H.Q. Visited in Company with D.A.D.V.S. 62nd Div. 2/2 (WR) Field Ambulance and all 62nd Div from. Evacuated twenty two animals, thirteen from Horse 62nd Division, General Routine of Section	S.R.B.
	3-10-17		Visited 2/1 and 2/2 Field Ambulances. Evacuated Horse 628 Coy General Routine of Section	S.R.B.
	4-10-17		General Routine of Section. Visited DHQ and HP R.E. 9 R.A. also Brigade Coys 9 Div France.	S.R.B.
	5-10-17		General Routine of Section. Visited DHQ and Signals. Visited 9 A.D.V.S.	S.R.B.
	6-10-17		General Routine of Section. Visited DHQ and Divisional France, and 2/1 and 2/(WR) Field Ambulances.	S.R.B.
	7-10-17		General Routine of Section. Visited DHQ and 528 Coy Div France,	S.R.B.
	8-10-17		General routine of Section. Visited V.O. Signals and 2/2 Field Ambulance.	S.R.B.
	9-10-17		General routine of Section. Visited new quarters of M.V.S. Pte Sykes 10.T.O.326.S. Became a Casualty	S.R.B.

Army Form C. 2118.

WAR DIARY
or
INTELLIGENCE SUMMARY
(Erase heading not required.)

2/1 (WR) M.V.S.

Instructions regarding War Diaries and Intelligence Summaries are contained in F.S. Regs., Part II. and the Staff Manual respectively. Title pages will be prepared in manuscript.

2/1st (W.R.) MOBILE VETERINARY SECTION.
No. M/1833
Date 2/11/17

Place	Date	Hour	Summary of Events and Information	Remarks and references to Appendices
	10-10-17		Proceeded on leave handed over M.V.S. to Capt Goff member A.V.C.	SLC
Larient	10/10/17		Capt Goff proceeded on leave took over command of section.	ym
	11/10/17		Routine of section. Visited 312 Brigade R.F.A.	ym
Marquid	12/10/17		Moved to Marquid. Attended over two evacuation cases to "B" mobile Vet. Section.	ym
	13/10/17		Received seven animals from "B" mobile V. Section.	ym
			Arranged fatigue work of section. Visited 157 Army no By. 461 R.S. 2/3 Field Amb. 702 + 201 M.G. Co. 12 Bn. Been attached from 22 Vety Hospital Boilers 12 a.s. been sent to Sn 2 Vety B officers ffo.	
	14/10/17		Routine work of section. Visited by DDV.S.	ym
	15/10/17		Routine of section. Visited 155 By Brigade 410 R.E. 2/1 Field Amb 0212 M.G. Co. A.T.C.	ym
	16/10/17		Routine of section. Evacuated 7 animals to "B" mobile Vet. Section. Visited to	ym
	17/10/17		155 By Brigade 411 R.E. 526 v 528 Co. A.T.C.	ym
	18/10/17		Routine of section. Visited 15C By Brigade 2/1 Field Amb. 212 M.G. Co.	ym
			Routine of section. Visit by DADV.S. Visit 185 By Brigade and D.A.D. vet returned	ym
	19/10/17		Routine of section. Admitted 3 horses. Visited 157 By Brigade 411 R.E. 526 v 528 Co.	ym
	20/10/17		Routine of section. Visited 2/6 v 528 Co. A.T.C. ADVS visited section	ym

T.2134. Wt. W708-776. 50C000. 4/15. Sir J.C. & S.

Army Form C. 2118.

WAR DIARY
or
INTELLIGENCE SUMMARY.
(Erase heading not required.)

2/1st (W.R.) Mob. Veterinary Section

Place	Date	Hour	Summary of Events and Information	Remarks
메린	21/10/17		Routine of section. Visited 187 Inf Bde 208 M.G.Co. 461 R.E. 2/3 Field Amb.	JM
	22/10/17		Church service by senior Chaplain. Arrival of hay & bran & forage.	JM
			Routine of section. Visited by ADVS + AA & QMG 62nd Division. Received 3 animals	JM
			Visited 2/1 A.S.C. P.M. on 208 M.G.Co. mule	JM
	23/10/17		Evacuated 6 animals. Horse used in Vet. Amb.	DTS
	23/10/17		2nd Lt. out section from Capt Martin arr. Visited 187th Brigade Group.	DTS
	24/10/17		Routine of Section. Visited E.A. DTS and 185th Brigade Group.	DTS
	25/10/17		Routine of section. Visited D.R. R.V.T. and 526 Corps Hd.	DTS
	26/10/17		Routine of Section. Visited S.A. DTS and 187 Brigade Group, and 2 Cy. A.S.C.	DTS
	27/10/17		Routine of Section. Visited 187 Brigade Group and S.A. DTS 36 Division made	DTS
			arrangements for evacuating animals until 48th M.V.C.	DTS
	28-10-17		Routine of Section. Visited 187 Brigade Group. L. Cpl Roberts entered C.R.S.	DTS
	29-10-17		Routine of Section. Visited See Paire.	DTS
	30-10-17		Moved to Courcelles.	DTS
	31-10-17		Moved to Merchelit. Visited E.R. DTS.	DTS

J.R. Crabb Capt avc (T)

ORIGINAL

Confidential
War Diary
of
2/1st (WR) Mobile Veterinary Section
From November 1st/17 To November 30th/17.

Volume XI.

S.R. Crabb
Capt AVC (TF)
O.C 2/1 (WR) M V.S

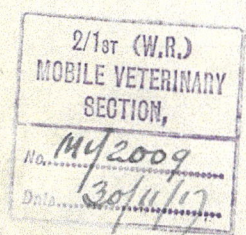

Army Form C. 2118.

WAR DIARY
or
INTELLIGENCE SUMMARY.
(Erase heading not required.)

2/1 (W.R.) Mobile Veterinary Section.

Place	Date	Hour	Summary of Events and Information	Remarks and references to Appendices
Monchiet	1-11-17		General routine of Section. Visited 2/4 & 2/5 K.O.Y.L.I. 2/4 and 2/5 D. of W. Lancs.	
	2-11-17		Visited 2/4 and 2/5 Duke of Wellingtons. 306 and 213 M.G. Coy. and 2/3 Field Ambulance. Visited D.A.D.V.S.	O.R.C.
	3-11-17		General routine of Section. Visited 2/3 Field Ambulance. 208 & 213 M.G. Coy.	O.R.C.
			General routine of Section. Visited 2/4 & 2/5 Duke of Wellingtons all 187 Brigade. & 2/5 Hussars.	O.R.C.
			and 208 & 213 M.G. Coy.	
	4-11-17		General routine of Section. Visited 213 & 208 M.G.C. 187 Brigade and 2/3 Field Ambulance. O.R.C.	O.R.C.
	5-11-17		General routine of Section. Paid men. Pte Roberts returned from E.R.S. Unless 273407 Pte ...	
	6-11-17		General routine of Section. Visited 2/4 and 2/5 D. of Wellingtons and 208 M.G. & Coy. 2/5 Lyly Byrd.	O.R.3
			also 2/3 (W.R.) Field Ambulance and 208 M.G. Coy. Pte Roberts returned to duty.	O.R.C.
	7-11-17		General Review. Visited 2/3 (W.R.) Field Ambulance and 2/4 & 2/5 D/W and S.E.C.	O.R.C.
	8-11-17		General Review of Section. No 6.2739 Pte Luciani C reported from 2/5 D/W for duty for duty	O.R.C.
			and No 261309 Pte Scully C evacuated to Base. Visited by and Visited by 2/4 S.F.B.	
9-11-17			General Review of Section. Visited 2/5 Field Ambulance and 2/5 Lyly Byrd	O.R.C.
			and 526 Coy A.S.C. also 213 & 212 M.G. Coy.	

2/1st (W.R.) MOBILE VETERINARY SECTION

Army Form C. 2118.

WAR DIARY
or
INTELLIGENCE SUMMARY.
(Erase heading not required.)

2/1 (W.R.) Mobile Veterinary Section.

Place	Date	Hour	Summary of Events and Information	Remarks and references to Appendices
Menchecourt	10-11-17		Visited D.A.D.V.S. General routine of section. Visited 2/5 and 2/6 W.R. Fd Ambs and 2/6 and 2/6 Duke of Wellingtons.	S.T.E.
	11-11-17		General routine of Section. Pte Lee entered hospital with P.U.O. Visited by D.A.D.V.S. Noticed 326 Coy 62nd Div horse 3/2 M.G. Coy and 2/7 and 2/6 West Yorks. also 2/4 and 2/6 Duke of Wellingtons.	S.T.E.
	12-11-17		Visited by D.A.D.V.S. General Routine of Section. Mules 326 Coy Feb also 2/4 Duke of Wellington.	S.T.E.
	13-11-17		Section moved to Achiet-le-Petit.	D.T.L.
Achiet-le-Petit	14-11-17		Evacuated 9 animals all 42nd Division. Section moved to Bancourt.	D.T.L.
Bancourt	15-11-17		Section double up with 1/1 London M.V. S.S.F. 17721 Pte Gallogoli W. entered hospt 2 M.Y. E.	D.T.L.
M.Y. Central	16-11-17		Evacuated 1 mule. Ordinary Routine of Section.	S.T.E.
	17-11-17		Ordinary routine of Section.	S.T.E.
	18-11-17		Visited by D.A.D.V.S. Ordinary routine of Section.	S.T.E.
	19-11-17		Pte S.F. 88 57 Pte Lee W. Evacuated to Base Hospital Rouen S.E.2063 Pte James W.R. Sick for duty from No 2 Veterinary Hospital, ordinary Routine of Section	S.T.E.
M.V.2009	20-11-17		Evacuated 32 animals 11.9.62 Div ? 21 other units "mange of the Mule"	S.T.E.
	30-11-17		Pte T. 752337 H. Knight entered 119 Field Ambulance	S.T.E.

2/1st (W.R.) MOBILE VETERINARY SECTION.

WAR DIARY
or
INTELLIGENCE SUMMARY.

Army Form C. 2118.

2/1st M.V.S.

Place	Date	Hour	Summary of Events and Information	Remarks and references to Appendices
McCuloch	21-11-17		Section Inspection & General M.O.C. Ordinary routine of Section	T.R.C.
	22-11-17		T.T. no 03207 Pte Roberts entered 2/2 London Field Ambulance ordinary routine of Section	T.R.C.
	23-11-17		Evacuated 6 animals, 102nd Div (sung) & 5th Mtd Brigade. Ordinary routine of Section	T.R.C.
	24-11-17		General Routine of Section	T.R.C.
	25-11-17		General Routine of Section. No SE 17721 Pte Holford W. evacuated to CCS (SI.)	T.R.C.
	26-11-17		General Routine of Section. Visited by ADVS IV Corps.	T.R.C.
	27-11-17		Evacuated 12 animals. 3 to "S" in. 1 to "M" in. 1 to 2 Mange Visited by ADVS IV Corps A.D.V.S. D.R.P.	DRP
	27-11-17		Routine of Section. Visited by ADVS 3rd Army	DE
	28-11-17		Routine of Section Visited by ADVS IV Corps. Sgt Holford W. attended CCS 44 Pt Rose	T.R.C.
	29-11-17		Routine of Section.	S.R.C.
	30-11-17		Routine of Section. Evacuated 20 animals. 4 to 2 Division.	

M. Wright Capt a/c

2/1st (W.R.)
MOBILE VETERINARY
SECTION.
No. MV2009
30/11/17

Vol 12

Secret

War Diary of
2/1 (WR) Mobile Veterinary Section.

for December. 1917

2/1st (W.R.)
MOBILE VETERINARY
SECTION.
No. M.V./2215
Date 1—12/17

D R Crabb Capt A.V.C (T.F)
O C 2/1 (WR) M.V.S.

Original

Army Form C. 2118.

WAR DIARY
or
INTELLIGENCE SUMMARY.
(Erase heading not required.) 2/1 (W.R.) Mobile Veterinary Section

Instructions regarding War Diaries and Intelligence Summaries are contained in F. S. Regs., Part II. and the Staff Manual respectively. Title pages will be prepared in manuscript.

Stamp: 2/1st (W.R.) MOBILE VETERINARY SECTION. No. MVS 22/5 Date 31-12-17

Place	Date	Hour	Summary of Events and Information	Remarks and references to Appendices
Bapaume	1-12-17		General Routine of Section	FRB
	2-12-17		General Routine of Section. Camp bombed. Corporal Beelow wounded & Admitted to 29 C.C.S.	FRB
	3-12-17		General Routine of Section.	FRB
	4-12-17		General Routine of Section. Evacuated 36 Animals, 4 of 62nd Division. Section moved to Bullecourt	FRB
Bullecourt	5-12-17		General Routine of Section.	FRB
	6-12-17		General Routine of Section. Section moved to Gouzeaucourt.	FRB
Gouzeaucourt	7-12-17		General Routine of Section.	FRB
	8-12-17		General Routine of Section.	FRB
	9-12-17		General Routine of Section.	FRB
	10-12-17		General Routine of Section.	FRB
	11-12-17		General Routine of Section. Section Inspected.	FRB
	12-12-17		General Routine of Section. Evacuated 8 Animals, all 62nd Div. 4 Mange.	FRB
	13-12-17		General Routine of Section. Pte 2063 Pte Jones entered 42 C.C.S.	FRB
	14-12-17		General Routine of Section. Section moved to Labeuvrière.	FRB
Labeuvrière	15-12-17		General Routine of Section.	FRB
	16-12-17		General Routine of Section.	FRB

J.M. Webb Capt

Army Form C. 2118.

WAR DIARY
INTELLIGENCE SUMMARY

(Erase heading not required.) 2/1 (W.R.) Mobile Veterinary Section

Place	Date	Hour	Summary of Events and Information	Remarks and references to Appendices
Catourière	17-12-17		General Routine of Section	D2B
	18-12-17		Section moved to Tinques, one mule of 62nd Division evacuated	72B
	19-12-17		General Routine of Section	72B
	20-12-17		General Routine of Section	72B
	21-12-17		General Routine of Section	72B
	22-12-17		General Routine of Section	72B
	23-12-17		General Routine of Section	72B
	24-12-17		General Routine of Section	72B
	25-12-17		General Routine of Section	72B
	26-12-17		General Routine of Section, evacuated 10 animals, 2 mangy all 62nd Division	72B
	27-12-17		General Routine of Section, SS 16740 Pte Pedesta R.J. evac. at 2/2 (W.R.) Field Ambulance	DTB
	28-12-17		General Routine of Section	72B
	29-12-17		General Routine of Section, TT03224 Pte Stenson R. Eff. entered 2/2 (W.R.) Field Amb.	72B
	30-12-17		General Routine of Section, SE 2011 S/Sgt East 18 days from duty Vet. Hospital	72B
	31-12-17		General Routine of Section	72B

J.R. Cook, Capt. A.V.C.
o.c. 2/1 W.R. M.V.S.

War Diary

of

2/1 West Riding Field Ambulance 62nd Division

1st Jan 1918 — 31st Jan 1918

Vol XIII

Army Form C. 2118.

WAR DIARY
of
INTELLIGENCE SUMMARY.
(Erase heading not required.)

Instructions regarding War Diaries and Intelligence Summaries are contained in F. S. Regs., Part II. and the Staff Manual respectively. Title pages will be prepared in manuscript.

original

9/1 West Riding mobile Veterinary Section

Place	Date	Hour	Summary of Events and Information	Remarks and references to Appendices
Tincques	1-1-18		Routine of Section. No TT. 03224 Pte Stephenson evacuated to 47 CCS.	J.R.B.
"	2-1-18		Routine of Section. No 16740 Pte Podcatu evacuated to 47 CCS.	J.R.B.
"	3-1-18		Routine of Section	J.R.B.
"	4-1-18		Routine of Section. Evacuated eleven animals, 9 mange, 1 of 12th Division	J.R.B.
			No 17755 Pte Baldwin went on leave to England.	J.R.B.
"	5-1-18		Routine of Section	J.R.B.
"	6-1-18		Routine of Section	J.R.B.
"	7-1-18		Routine of Section. to 4207 Pte Phillips J. posted from No 2 B.V.H.	J.R.B.
"	8-1-18		Routine of Section	J.R.B.
"	9-1-18		Section moved to Anzin. Evacuated 4 animals of 62 Division	J.R.B.
Anzin	10-1-18		Routine of Section	J.R.B.
"	11-1-18		Routine of Section. Inspected by A.D.V.S. XIII Corps	J.R.B.
"	12-1-18		Evacuated fifteen animals with mange and eight for other causes	J.R.B.
"	13-1-18		Routine of Section	J.R.B.
"	14-1-18		Routine of Section	J.R.B.
"	15-1-18		Routine of Section. Evacuated twenty three animals, 9 from VIII Corps M.V.D.	J.R.B.

Army Form C. 2118.

WAR DIARY
of
INTELLIGENCE SUMMARY.

original

Of unit Being mobile veterinary Section

(Erase heading not required.)

Instructions regarding War Diaries and Intelligence Summaries are contained in F. S. Regs., Part II. and the Staff Manual respectively. Title pages will be prepared in manuscript.

Place	Date	Hour	Summary of Events and Information	Remarks and references to Appendices
Angers	16-1-18		Routine of Section.	M.R.S.
	17-1-18		Routine of Section.	M.R.S.
	18-1-18		Routine of Section	M.R.S.
	19-1-18		Routine of Section. Evacuated fourteen animals, six mange.	M.R.S.
	20-1-18		Routine of Section.	M.R.S.
	21-1-18		Routine of Section. No, 17753 Pte Baldwin returned from leave.	M.R.S.
	22-1-18		Routine of Section. No 16516 Pte Ca Ahdy departed on leave to England.	M.R.S.
	23-1-18		Routine of Section. Evacuated 14 animals, 3 mange. No 17158 and 30800 Pte Boswell H & Pte Boswell B, reposted from No 2 B.V.H.	M.R.S.
	24-1-18		Routine of Section.	M.R.S.
	25-1-18		Routine of Section.	M.R.S.
	26-1-18		Routine of Section.	M.R.S.
	27-1-18		Routine of Section. Evacuated 14 animals, 8 of 62nd Division, six of this unit.	M.R.S.
	28-1-18		Routine of Section	M.R.S.
	29-1-18		Routine of Section. Took over drawing of O.R.D.E.S.	M.R.S.
	30-1-18		Routine of Section. Evacuated 17 animals, 15 of 62 Div. 2 of this Unit.	M.R.S.
	31-1-18		Routine of Section	M.R.S.

L.M. Stapp
Capt
O.C. 2/1 WR M.V. Vet Section

Original

QR 14

Confidential
War Diary
of
21st (W.R.) Mobile Veterinary Section

1st February 1918
28th February 1918

Volume XIV

Army Form C. 2118.

WAR DIARY
INTELLIGENCE SUMMARY.

(Erase heading not required.)

Original

2/1 West Riding Mobile Veterinary Section.

Instructions regarding War Diaries and Intelligence Summaries are contained in F. S. Regs., Part II. and the Staff Manual respectively. Title pages will be prepared in manuscript.

Place	Date	Hour	Summary of Events and Information	Remarks and references to Appendices
Anzin	1-2-18		Commenced treatment of "Specific Ophthalmia" of ponies on completion with iodine.	SRB
"	2-2-18		Iodine treatment seems to have given favourable results in some cases, but given stim. Pte Rolfe detailed on leave to England.	TRB
"	3-2-18		Have again painted conjunctiva but this has given rise to a severe pain when on first session.	TRB
"	4-2-18		Accompanied ADVS XVIII Corps in an inspection of 312 Brigade R.F.A.	SRB
"	5-2-18		Have discontinued treatment of Ophthalmia with iod: iodine as upon it too severs & painful	SRB
"	6-2-18		Routine of Section	SRB
"	7-2-18		Evacuated 21 Animals 13 of 62nd Div. 8 of other units.	SRB
"	8-2-18		Routine of Section	SRB
"	9-2-18		Corporal Carber returned on leave to England also Pte Luke.	SRB
"	10-2-18		Routine of Section	SRB
"	11-2-18		Section moved to Vaudricourt.	SRB
Vaudricourt	12-2-18		Routine of Section	SRB
"	13-2-18		Evacuated 8 animals 3 of 62nd Division 8 of other Divisions	SRB

Army Form C. 2118.

WAR DIARY
INTELLIGENCE SUMMARY.
(Erase heading not required.) 2/1 (W.R.) Motor Veterinary Section

Instructions regarding War Diaries and Intelligence Summaries are contained in F.S. Regs., Part II. and the Staff Manual respectively. Title pages will be prepared in manuscript.

Place	Date	Hour	Summary of Events and Information	Remarks and references to Appendices
Vandincourt.	14-2-18		Review of Section	A.T.R.8.
	15-2-18		Routine of Section. Sergt. Mpetchin departure on leave to U.K.	A.T.R.8.
	16-2-18		Routine of Section. Pte Roff returned from leave.	A.T.R.8.
	17-2-18		Routine of Section. Evacuated 20 animals. Sick of 62nd Div. 15 of other formations	A.T.R.8.
	18-2-18		Routine of Section	A.T.R.8.
	19-2-18		Review of Section	A.T.R.8.
	20-2-18		Evacuated 8 animals. 1 of 62nd Div. 7 of other formations	A.T.R.8.
	21-2-18		Routine of Section	A.T.R.8.
	22-2-18		Routine of Section. Pte Cooker returned from leave.	A.T.R.8.
	23-2-18		Routine Section. Pte Soto returned from leave.	A.T.R.8.
	24-2-18		Routine of Section	A.T.R.8.
	25-2-18		Routine of Section. Evacuated 8 animals. 6 of 62nd Div. 2 of other animals	A.T.R.8.
	26-2-18		Routine of Section	A.T.R.8.
	27-2-18		Routine of Section	A.T.R.8.
	28-2-18		Routine of Section	A.T.R.8.

F.K. Cottrell
Captain R.A.V.C.
co 2/1(W.R.) M.V.S.

Original

27

Confidential

War Diary of

2/1 (WR) M.V.S

from 1-3-18 to 31-3-18

OC 2/1 WR MVS D.R. Crabb Captain

Vol XV

Confidential

Original

Army Form C. 2118.

WAR DIARY
or
INTELLIGENCE SUMMARY.
(Erase heading not required.)

of 21 (WR) Mobile Veterinary Section

Vol 15

Instructions regarding War Diaries and Intelligence Summaries are contained in F.S. Regs., Part II. and the Staff Manual respectively. Title pages will be prepared in manuscript.

Place	Date	Hour	Summary of Events and Information	Remarks and references to Appendices
Vandelicourt	1-3-18		Routine of Section.	
	2-3-18		Routine of Section. Sergt McPhee returned from leave. Pte Bird reported back on duty off Pte.	
	3-3-18		Routine of Section. Attended a board of Officers to scrutinise the mobilization stores table	SRG/STG
	4-3-18		Revised of Section. Section moved to Écurie Forth near XIII Corps Horse Depot	
Écurie	5-3-18		Handed over 2/(WR) M.V.S. to Capt Bryson A.V.C. (TF) proceeding on leave to Colonel McCullagh.	
	6-3-18		Routine of Section. Kept watch on the Evacuation returns from Isere No Dipping Dept being under Repair	mmfs
	7-3-18		Routine of Section. 7 Horses 14 Mules Evacuated 6 hrs/4 r.t.	mmfs
	8-3-18		Routine of Section.	mmfs
	9-3-18		Routine of Section. 3 Horses Evacuated 15 no 14 Hosp	mmfs
	10-3-18		Routine of Section. Pte Murrell proceeds on leave to U.K.	mmfs
	11-3-18		Routine of Section.	mmfs
	12-3-18		Routine of Section. 3 Horses & 2 Mules Evacuated 10 no 4 Vet. D. Knight returns BWK.	mmfs
	13-3-18		Routine of Section.	mmfs
	14-3-18		Routine of Section. Pte Lucione returns to duty	mmfs
	15-3-18		Routine of Section.	mmfs
	16-3-18		Routine of Section. 3 Horses & 2 Mules Evacuated 6 hrs/4 r.t. Pte Dutton on leave back.	mmfs

WAR DIARY
INTELLIGENCE SUMMARY

(Erase heading not required.) 2/1 or M.V.S. 62nd Division

Army Form C. 2118.

Place	Date	Hour	Summary of Events and Information	Remarks and references to Appendices
Ervie	17.3.18		Routine office	Nil
"	18.3.18		Routine office. 6 horses evacuated Nos 14, 15, 16 Burdell on leave U.K.	Nil
"	19.3.18		Routine office	Nil
"	20.3.18		Routine office	Nil
"	21.3.18		Routine office. 3 horses evacuated Nos 17,18. Cpl Bell relieved providing escort for sick horses	Nil
			Pte Best on leave to U.K. (hurt)	
"			Returned from town late our commenced f M.V.S. from Cpl. Bryan + V.C. Returned arrived at S.A.D.V.S. 62nd Division	SRB
"	22.3.18		General routine of section. Visited by A.D.V.S. VIII Corps. Evacuated 3 animals SRB	SRB
"	23.3.18		General routine of section. Visited by A.D.V.S. Pte Hetherington 3 days on the leave.	SRB
"			Remounted him (1 evacuee) sent to S.A.D.V.S. 62nd Division SRB	SRB
"	24.3.18		Evacuated 16 animals through H.S.A.D.V.S. Moved to Bertrancourt	SRB
"			Section arrived H.S.A.D.V.S. 62nd Division	SRB
Bertrancourt	25.3.18		General routine of section	SRB
"	26.3.18		General routine of section	SRB
"	27.3.18		General routine of section. 1 animal handed to 27 M.V.S.	SRB

Army Form C. 2118.

WAR DIARY
or
INTELLIGENCE SUMMARY.

(Erase heading not required.)

Original 2/1 (WR) M.V.S. 62nd Division.

Instructions regarding War Diaries and Intelligence Summaries are contained in F. S. Regs., Part II. and the Staff Manual respectively. Title pages will be prepared in manuscript.

Place	Date	Hour	Summary of Events and Information	Remarks and references to Appendices
Bonneville	26-3-18		General retiring of Section.	S&D
	29-3-18		General retiring of section.	D.R.E.
	30-3-18		Section moved to Thièvres. 3 animals evacuated.	D.R.E. S.P.B.
Thièvres	31-3-18		Routine of section.	S.P.B. D.R. Crabb Exps out (?) O.C. 2/(WR)M.V.S.
			2/1(WR)M.V.S. arrived in France on 12 Jan 1917. Strength Officers	

Original

CONFIDENTIAL

War Diary

of

2/1st West Riding Mobile Veterinary Section

1st April 1918 to 30th April 1918

Volume 16.

Original

Army Form C. 2118.

WAR DIARY
INTELLIGENCE SUMMARY.
2/1 West Riding Mobile Veterinary Section

(Erase heading not required.)

Instructions regarding War Diaries and Intelligence Summaries are contained in F. S. Regs., Part II. and the Staff Manual respectively. Title pages will be prepared in manuscript.

Place	Date	Hour	Summary of Events and Information	Remarks and references to Appendices
Thivres	1-4-18	—	Evacuated six animals to V.E. Station at Frevillers.	F.B.
"	2-4-18	—	General routine of Section.	F.B.
"	3-4-18		Section moved to Pas-en-Artois.	F.R.C.
Pas-en-Artois	4-4-18		General Routine of Section.	F.R.C.
"	5-4-18		General Routine of Section.	F.R.C.
"	6-4-18		Evacuated Ten animals to V.E. Station Frevillers.	F.R.C.
			Pvt. Holroyd W. tried and found guilty of Self General Cont medical, in on charge of King about three days without leave return on active service in the field.	F.B.
"	11-4-18		Station moved to Souastre.	F.B.
Souastre	8-4-18		Section moved to Henu, Pt. Holroyd. entered Hospital.	F.R.C.
Henu	9-4-18		Evacuated 10 animals to V.E. Station Frevillers.	F.R.C.
"	10-4-18		Evacuated Routine of Section	F.R.C.
"	11-4-18		Evacuated 24 animals to V.E. Station Boullens.	F.R.C.
"	12-4-18		Evacuated 16 animals to V.E. Station Boullens.	F.R.C.
"	13-4-18		Evacuated 16 animals to V.E. Station Boullens.	F.R.C.
"	14-4-18		Evacuated 12 animals to V.E. Station Boullens.	F.R.C.

Original

Army Form C. 2118.

WAR DIARY
INTELLIGENCE SUMMARY.
(Erase heading not required.)

of No 5 Mobile Veterinary Section

Instructions regarding War Diaries and Intelligence Summaries are contained in F. S. Regs., Part II. and the Staff Manual respectively. Title pages will be prepared in manuscript.

Place	Date	Hour	Summary of Events and Information	Remarks and references to Appendices
Henin	15-4-18		Evacuated 9 animals to V.E. Station Saulties.	M.V.
"	16-4-18		Pte Best returned from leave & U.K. Evacuated 14 animals to V.E. Station Saulties	M.V.S.
"	17-4-18		Section moved to Pas - en - Artois.	M.V.S.
Pas en Artois	18-4-18		Arrival of Section.	M.V.S.
	19-4-18		Evacuated 10 animals to V.E. Station Saulties. Pte Rolfe entered Hospital.	M.V.S.
	20-4-18		Evacuated 12 animals to V.E. Station Saulties. Pte Lucienne returned from leave.	M.V.S.
	21-4-18		Evacuated 9 animals to V.E. Station Saulties. Pte Lucienne entered Hospital.	M.V.S.
	22-4-18		Evacuated 10 animals to V.E. Station Saulties.	M.V.S.
	23-4-18		Evacuated 10 animals to V.E. Station Saulties. Pte Wright, Pte Bradley & Pte Carlyle to Hospital.	M.V.S.
	24-4-18		Evacuated 15 animals to V.E. Station Saulties. Pte Woodland reported for duty from No 2 Vety Hospital.	M.V.S.
	25-4-18		Evacuated 12 animals TV.E. Station. Pte Benard returned from leave London escort.	M.V.S.
	26-4-18		Evacuated animals to V.E.S. Pte Luke left section for No 2 Vety Hospital. Pte Bailey Reported for duty.	M.V.S.
	27-4-18		Evacuated 7 animals to V.E. Station Saulties.	M.V.S.
	28-4-18		Evacuated 11 animals to V.E. Station Saulties. S-gt Walton left for No 2 Vet Hospital for transfer to England.	M.V.S.
	29-4-18		Evacuated 7 animals to V.E.S Saulties.	M.V.S.
	30-4-19		Evacuated 15 animals to V.E. Saulties. Pte Duckworth admitted to Hospital	M.V.S.

S.R. Crabb Capt & over
O.C. 2/(NR) M.V.S.

WAR DIARY
or
INTELLIGENCE SUMMARY.

Army Form C. 2118.

Original

2/1 West Riding Mobile Veterinary Section

Place	Date	Hour	Summary of Events and Information	Remarks and references to Appendices
Pas-en-Artois	1-5-18		Evacuated 9 animals to No 5 V.E.S.	S.R.6.
	2-5-18		Routine of Section.	J.R.6.
	3-5-18		Evacuated 6 animals to No 5 V.E.S. 3rd Shropshire Yeo relieved from 62 Division.	D.R.6.
	4-5-18		No 19943 Pte Bousall Wr tried by J.G.C.M. and sentenced to 21 days F.P. No 2.	J.R.6.
			Routine of Section.	J.R.6.
	5-5-18		Evacuated 2 animals to No 5 V.E.S.	J.R.6.
	6-5-18		Evacuated 8 animals to No 5 V.E.S.	J.R.6.
	7-5-18		Evacuated 13 animals to No 5 V.E.S.	D.R.6.
	8-5-18		Routine of Section.	D.R.6.
	9-5-18		8 animals evacuated to No 5 V.E.S.	J.R.6.
	10-5-18		Routine of Section.	J.R.6.
	11-5-18		Evacuated 12 animals to No 5 V.E.S.	J.R.6.
	12-5-18		Routine of Section.	D.R.6.
	13-5-18		Evacuated 13 animals to No 5 V.E.S.	J.R.6.
	14-5-18		Routine of Section.	J.R.6.
	15-5-18		Evacuated 10 animals to No 5 V.E.S.	J.R.6.

J.R. Cobb Capt and (V.C.)

Army Form C. 2118.

WAR DIARY
or
INTELLIGENCE SUMMARY.

(Erase heading not required.) 2/(or) Mobile Veterinary Section

Original

Instructions regarding War Diaries and Intelligence Summaries are contained in F. S. Regs., Part II. and the Staff Manual respectively. Title pages will be prepared in manuscript.

Place	Date	Hour	Summary of Events and Information	Remarks and references to Appendices
Pas-en-Artois	16-5-18		Sergt Hill A/VO Reported for duty from England.	
"	17-5-18		Routine of Section.	J.R.C.
"	18-5-18		Evacuated 10 animals to No 3 V.E.S. Staff Sergt Peck sent to the 2 Vet Hospital.	J.R.C.
"	19-5-18		Routine of Section.	J.R.C.
"	20-5-18		Routine of Section.	J.R.C.
"	21-5-18		Routine of Section.	J.R.C.
"	22-5-18		Pte Hollings returned from hospital.	J.R.C.
"	23-5-18		Routine of Section.	J.R.C.
"	25-5-18		Routine of Section. Pte Brett sent to the 2 Vet Hospital.	J.R.C.
"	26-5-18		Routine of Section.	J.R.C.
"	27-5-18		Routine of Section.	J.R.C.
"	28-5-18		Evacuated 33 animals to No 4 V.E.S.	J.R.C.
"	29-5-18		Evacuated 8 animals to the 4 V.E.S. The Battery sent to the 2 Vet Hospital.	J.R.C.
"	30-5-18		Evacuated 6 animals to the 4 V.E.S.	J.R.C.
"	31-5-18		Evacuated 5 animals to the 4 V.E.S.	J.R.C.

J.R. Cobb Capt AVC (TF)
O C 2/(or) M.V.S.

CONFIDENTIAL

WAR DIARY

OF

2/1st WEST RIDING MOBILE VETERINARY SERVICES.

From 1st June to 30th June 1915

Volume XVIII

Army Form C. 2118.

Original

WAR DIARY
or
INTELLIGENCE SUMMARY.
(Erase heading not required.)

2/1 (West Riding) Mobile Veterinary Section

Instructions regarding War Diaries and Intelligence Summaries are contained in F. S. Regs., Part II. and the Staff Manual respectively. Title pages will be prepared in manuscript.

Place	Date	Hour	Summary of Events and Information	Remarks and references to Appendices
Pas-en-Artois	1-6-15		Evacuated 3 animals to No 4 V.E.S.	J.R.C.
"	2-6-15		Evacuated 6 animals to No 4 V.E.S	J.R.C.
"	3-6-15		Nothing to Report	J.R.C.
"	4-6-15		Nothing to Report	J.R.C.
"	5-6-15		12 animals Evacuated to No 4 V.E.S.	J.R.C.
"	6-6-15		Nothing to Report	J.R.C.
"	7-6-15		Nothing to Report	J.R.C.
"	8-6-15		15 animals Evacuated to No 4 V.E.S.	J.R.C.
"	9-6-15		2 animals Evacuated to No 4 V.E.S.	J.R.C.
"	10-6-15		Nothing to Report	J.R.C.
"	11-6-15		Nothing to Report	J.R.C.
"	12-6-15		Nothing to Report	J.R.C.
"	13-6-15		13 animals Evacuated to No 4 V.E.S	J.R.C.
"	14-6-15		2 animals Evacuated to No 4 V.E.S	J.R.C.
"	15-6-15		8 animals Evacuated to No 4 V.E.S	J.R.C.
"	16-6-15		Nothing to Report	J.R.C.

J.R.C. Captain A.V.O. (T.F.)
2/1 (W. R.) Mobile Veterinary Section

Army Form C. 2118.

WAR DIARY
~~INTELLIGENCE SUMMARY.~~
(Erase heading not required.)   2/1 West Riding Mobile Vet. Section.

Instructions regarding War Diaries and Intelligence Summaries are contained in F. S. Regs., Part II. and the Staff Manual respectively. Title pages will be prepared in manuscript.

Original

Place	Date	Hour	Summary of Events and Information	Remarks and references to Appendices
Pas-en-Artois	17-6-18		28 animals Evacuated to No 4 V.E.S.	J.R.C.
	18-6-18		Nothing to Report	J.R.C.
	19-6-18		Nothing to Report	J.R.C.
	20-6-18		Nothing to Report	J.R.C.
	21-6-18		Nothing to Report	J.R.C.
	22-6-18		22 animals Evacuated to No 4 V.E.S.	J.R.C.
	23-6-18		1 animal Evacuated to No 4 V.E.S.	J.R.C.
	24-6-18		2 animals Evacuated to No 4 V.E.S.	J.R.C.
	25-6-18		Nothing to Report	J.R.C.
	26-6-18		2 animals Evacuated to No 4 V.E.S.	J.R.C.
	27-6-18		Nothing to Report	J.R.C.
	28-6-18		7 animals Evacuated to No 4 V.E.S.	J.R.C.
	29-6-18		Nothing to Report	J.R.C.
	30-6-18		Nothing to Report	J.R.C.

J.R. Cash
CAPTAIN A. V. C. (T. F.)
O. C. 2/1 (W. R.) MOBILE VETERINARY SECTION

Confidential

War Diary

of

1/1st (West Riding) Mobile Veterinary Section

From 1st July 1918 to 31st July 1918

Volume 19

Army Form C. 2118.

WAR DIARY
or
INTELLIGENCE SUMMARY

(Erase heading not required.) Original 4/(?) Mobile Veterinary Section

Instructions regarding War Diaries and Intelligence Summaries are contained in F. S. Regs., Part II. and the Staff Manual respectively. Title pages will be prepared in manuscript.

Place	Date	Hour	Summary of Events and Information	Remarks and references to Appendices
Pozo del Aisa	1-7-18	—	4 animals evacuated to 4 M.V.S	
	2-7-18	—	Nothing to Report	520
	3-7-18	—	Nothing to Report	520
	4-7-18	—	Nothing to Report	520
	5-7-18	—	8 animals evacuated to 4th M.V.S.	520
	6-7-18	—	Nothing to Report	520
	7-7-18	—	Nothing to Report	520
	8-7-18	—	Nothing to Report	S.R.C.
	9-7-18	—	Nothing to Report	S.R.C.
	10-7-18	—	7 animals evacuated to 4 M.V.S. no 4.	S.R.C.
	11-7-18	—	Nothing to Report.	S.R.C.
	12-7-18	—	Nothing to Report.	S.R.C.
	13-7-18	—	Nothing to Report.	S.R.C.
	14-7-18	—	14 animals handed over to 39 Division. Section entrained	S.R.C.
	15-7-18	—	Nothing to Report.	S.R.C.
Noulhy	16-7-18	—	Section at Noulhy	S.R.C.

Army Form C. 2118.

WAR DIARY
or
INTELLIGENCE SUMMARY.
(Erase heading not required.)

Orig. 21 (4CR) Motor Delivery Section

Date	Hour	Summary of Events and Information	Remarks and references to Appendices
May 17-7-18	—	Section moved to Crevic sur Coole.	
Crevic 18-7-18	—	Section moved to Toul sur Marne.	
Toul 19-7-18	—	Nothing to Report.	
Toul 20-7-18	—	Section moved to Germaine.	
Germaine 21-7-18	—	Nothing to Report.	
22-7-18	—	Nothing to Report.	
23-7-18	—	Nothing to Report.	
24-7-18	—	Nothing to Report.	
25-7-18	—	Nothing to Report.	
26-7-18	—	Nothing to Report.	
27-7-18	—	Nothing to Report.	
28-7-18	—	Nothing to Report.	
29-7-18	—	Evacuated 15 animals to No 23 M.V.S.	
30-7-18	—	Nothing to Report.	
31-7-18	—	Nothing to Report.	

J.R. Crabb
Capt. ver. (T.F)
OC 21 (4CR) M.V.S.

CONFIDENTIAL.

ORIGINAL.

WAR DIARY.

OF

2/1st. W. R. MOBILE VETERINARY SECTION

VOLUME XX

From 1st August, 1918.
To 31st August, 1918.

Army Form C. 2118.

WAR DIARY
INTELLIGENCE SUMMARY.
(Erase heading not required.)

2/1 (M.R) Mobile Veterinary Section

Instructions regarding War Diaries and Intelligence Summaries are contained in F. S. Regs., Part II. and the Staff Manual respectively. Title pages will be prepared in manuscript.

Place	Date	Hour	Summary of Events and Information	Remarks and references to Appendices
Germaine	1-8-18		Moved Section to Bicaruil	J.R.6.
Bicaruil	2-8-18		Nothing to report	J.R.6.
"	3-8-18		Nothing to report	J.R.6.
Vertios	4-8-18		Entrained Section at Vertios	J.R.6.
Candas	5-8-18		Detrained at Candas & section marched to Saston	J.R.6.
Saston	6-8-18		Nothing to report	J.R.6.
"	7-8-18		Evacuated 5 animals to No 4 V.E.S.	J.R.6.
"	8-8-18		Nothing to report	J.R.6.
"	9-8-18		Evacuated 16 animals to No 4 V.E.S.	J.R.6.
"	10-8-18		Evacuated 18 animals to No 4 V.E.S.	J.R.6.
"	11-8-18		Evacuated 6 animals to No 4 V.E.S.	J.R.6.
"	12-8-18		Nothing to report	J.R.6.
"	13-8-18		No 76701 Pte Richardson P.S., No 114329 Pte Taylor F., No 30711 Pte Weston reported from No 2 C.H.D.	J.R.6.
"	14-8-18		Evacuated 6 animals to No 4 V.E.S.	J.R.6.
"	15-8-18		No 03283 Cpl Casper, No 17721 Pte Holroyd W., 17755 Pte Baldwin G. dispatched to the 2 Vet Hospital	J.R.6.
"	16-8-18		Evacuated 6 animals to No 4 V.E.S. No 4201 Pte Philips on leave to U.K.	J.R.6.

Army Form C. 2118.

WAR DIARY
or
INTELLIGENCE SUMMARY.
(Erase heading not required.) 2/1 (W.R.) Mobile Veterinary Section

Instructions regarding War Diaries and Intelligence Summaries are contained in F.S. Regs., Part II. and the Staff Manual respectively. Title pages will be prepared in manuscript.

Place	Date	Hour	Summary of Events and Information	Remarks and references to Appendices
Sarton	17-5-18		Nothing to report	S.R.6.
"	18-5-18		Evacuated 4 animals to No 4 V.E.S.	S.R.6.
Saulty	19-5-18		Evacuated 13 animals to No 4 V.E.S. Section moved to Saulty	S.R.6.
"	20-5-18		Nothing to report	S.R.6.
"	21-5-18		Moved to Sarton	S.R.6.
Sarton	22-5-18		Nothing to report	S.R.6.
Saulty	23-5-18		1 animal evacuated sicken. Moved to Saulty. Cpl Cooper returned for rest. H/Sgt	S.R.6.
Bienvillers	24-5-18		3 animals evacuated to No 6. V.E.S. Section moved to Bienvillers	S.R.6.
"	25-5-18		Established advanced post at Douchy. No. 10760 Pte Woodland sent to No 2 Vety Hospital	S.R.6.
"	26-5-18		Nothing to report	S.R.6.
"	27-5-18		Nothing to report	S.R.6.
"	28-5-18		Nothing to report	S.R.6.
"	29-5-18		14 animals evacuated to No 6 V.E.S.	S.R.6.
"	30-5-18		9 animals evacuated to No 6 V.E.S.	S.R.6.
Douchy les Ayette	31		Section moved to Douchy les Ayette	

J.R. Cobb
CAPTAIN A. V. C. (T.F.)
O. C. 2/1 (W. R.) MOBILE VETERINARY SECTION

CONFIDENTIAL.

ORIGINAL.

WAR DIARY.

OF

2/1st. W. R. MOBILE VETERINARY SECTION

VOLUME XX

From 1st August, 1918.
To 31st August, 1918.

Confidential

War Diary
of
2/9 (N.R.) Mobile Veterinary Section

1st Sept 1918 — 30th Sept 1918

Volume XXI

Army Form C. 2118.

Original

WAR DIARY
or
INTELLIGENCE SUMMARY.

(Erase heading not required.) 2/3 (A.R.) Mobile Veterinary Section.

Instructions regarding War Diaries and Intelligence Summaries are contained in F. S. Regs., Part II. and the Staff Manual respectively. Title pages will be prepared in manuscript.

Place	Date	Hour	Summary of Events and Information	Remarks and references to Appendices
Donchy-la-pôte	1-9-18		Advanced aid post established at Guuicourt	D.R.E.
	2-9-18		16 animals evacuated to No 6 V.E.S. Pte Philip returned from leave	D.R.E.
	3-9-18		4 animals evacuated to No 6 V.E.S.	D.R.E.
Guuicourt	4-9-18		11 animals evacuated to No 6 V.E.S. Section moved to Guuicourt	D.R.E.
	5-9-18		Nothing to report.	D.R.E.
	6-9-18		Nothing to report.	D.R.E.
	7-9-18		9 animals evacuated to No 4 V.E.S.	D.R.E.
	8-9-18		Nothing to report.	M.E.
	9-9-18		12 animals evacuated to No 4 V.E.S.	D.R.E.
	10-9-18		Section moved to Gouricourt	D.R.E.
Gouricourt	11-9-18		Nothing to report	D.R.E.
	12-9-18		Nothing to report.	D.R.E.
	13-9-18		3 animals evacuated to No 4 V.E.S.	M.E.
	14-9-18		9 animals evacuated to No 4 V.E.S.	D.R.E.
	15-9-18		1 animal evacuated to No 4 V.E.S.	D.R.E.
	16-9-18		6 animals evacuated to No 4 V.E.S. Section moved to Gouricourt	D.R.E.

T2134. Wt. W708—776. 50C000. 4/15. Sir J. C. & S.

Army Form C. 2118.

Original

WAR DIARY
INTELLIGENCE SUMMARY.

(Erase heading not required.)

2/1 (2/W.R.) Mobile Veterinary Section

Instructions regarding War Diaries and Intelligence Summaries are contained in F. S. Regs., Part II. and the Staff Manual respectively. Title pages will be prepared in manuscript.

Place	Date	Hour	Summary of Events and Information	Remarks and references to Appendices
Lamincourt	17-9-18		Nothing to Report.	SPC
"	18-9-18		Nothing to Report.	SPC
"	19-9-18		3 animals evacuated to No 7 V.E.S. Pte Dennis on leave to U.K.	SPC
"	20-9-18		4 animals evacuated to No 4 V.E.S.	SPC
"	21-9-18		Nothing to Report.	SPC
"	22-9-18		2 animals evacuated to No 4 V.E.S.	SPC
"	23-9-18		Nothing to Report.	SPC
"	24-9-18		6 animals evacuated to No 4 V.E.S.	SPC
"	25-9-18		3 animals evacuated to No 4 V.E.S.	SPC
Bertincourt	26-9-18		Section moved to Bertincourt. Cpl Carter on leave to U.K.	SPC
"	27-9-18		Nothing to Report.	SPC
"	28-9-18		3 animals evacuated to No 5 V.E.S.	SPC
Hermies	29-9-18		2 animals evacuated to No 5 V.E.S. Section moved to Hermies.	SPC
"	30-9-18		Nothing to Report.	SPC

J. R. Crabb Capt. A.V.C. (T.)
O.C. 2/1 (2/W) M.V.S.

No. 23

Confidential

War Diary

of

9th K.R. Met. Telemmy Sec-

Oct 31st 1918

b

Volume XXIV

Original

28031 W3125/M2250 1000m 6/17 M.R.Co.,Ltd. (1367) Forms W3091.   Army Form W. 3091.

Cover for Documents.

Natures of Enclosures.

Notes, or Letters written.

Army Form C. 2118.

WAR DIARY
or
INTELLIGENCE SUMMARY.

(Erase heading not required.)

21 (aux) Mobile Veterinary Section

Instructions regarding War Diaries and Intelligence Summaries are contained in F. S. Regs., Part II. and the Staff Manual respectively. Title pages will be prepared in manuscript.

& Original

Place	Date	Hour	Summary of Events and Information	Remarks and references to Appendices
Mexico	1-10-18		29 animals evacuated to No 3 V.E.S.	✓
"	2-10-18		29 animals evacuated to No 4 V.E.S.	F.P.B.
"	3-10-18		14 animals evacuated to No 4 V.E.S.	F.P.B.
"	4-10-18		12 animals evacuated to No 4 V.E.S.	F.P.B.
"	5-10-18		12 animals evacuated to No 4 V.E.S.	F.P.B.
"	6-10-18		12 animals evacuated to No 6 V.E.S.	F.P.B.
"	7-10-18		9 animals evacuated to No 6 V.E.S.	F.P.B.
"	8-10-18		20 animals evacuated to No 6 V.E.S.	F.P.B.
Maurecourt	9-10-18		Section moved to Maurecourt	F.P.B.
Maurecourt	10-10-18		Section moved to Maisnieres	F.P.B.
Senainville	11-10-18		Section moved to Senainville	F.P.B.
"	12-10-18		Nothing to report	F.P.B.
"	13-10-18		21 animals evacuated to No 6 V.E.S.	F.P.B.
Catterine	14-10-18		Section moved to Catterine	F.P.B.
"	15-10-18		Noting to report	F.P.B.
Quesnoy Farm	16-10-18		Section moved to Quesnoy Farm	F.P.B.

J.R. Giles Capt AVC
O.C. 21 (aux) M.V.S.

Army Form C. 2118.

WAR DIARY
or
INTELLIGENCE SUMMARY.

(Erase heading not required.) 2/1 (W.R.) M.V.R.

2 Original

Instructions regarding War Diaries and Intelligence Summaries are contained in F. S. Regs., Part II. and the Staff Manual respectively. Title pages will be prepared in manuscript.

Place	Date	Hour	Summary of Events and Information	Remarks and references to Appendices
Feary Farm	17-10-14		Nothing to Report.	DRC
	18-10-14		Nothing to Report.	DRC
	19-10-14		19 animals evacuated to 6 V.E.S.	DRC
	20-10-14		Nothing to Report.	DRC
	21-10-14		16 animals evacuated to 6 V.E.S.	DRC
	22-10-14		Nothing to Report.	DRC
	23-10-14		23 animals evacuated to 6 V.E.S.	DRC
	24-10-14		Nothing to Report.	DRC
	25-10-14		5 animals evacuated to 6 V.E.S.	DRC
	26-10-14		2 animals evacuated to 6 V.E.S.	DRC
	27-10-14		Nothing to Report.	DRC
	28-10-14		3 animals evacuated to 6 V.E.S.	DRC
	29-10-14		19 animals evacuated to 6 V.E.S.	DRC
	30-10-14		Section moved to Tester Jonkine Farm	DRC
Tester Jonk	31-10-14			

J.R. Cate
CAPTAIN A.V.C. (T.F.)
O.C. 2/1 (W.R.) MOBILE VETERINARY SECTION

CONFIDENTIAL

War Diary

of

9/st (N.R.) Mobile Veterinary Section

Nov 1st 1918 to Nov. 30th 1918

VOLUME XXIII

No 24

Original

28031 W3125/M2250 1000m 6/17 M.R.Co.,Ltd. (1367) Forms W3091.

Army Form W.3091.

Cover for Documents.

Natures of Enclosures.

Notes, or Letters written.

Army Form C. 2118.

Original 2/1 (n.R) Mob. Vet. Section

WAR DIARY or INTELLIGENCE SUMMARY.

(Erase heading not required.)

Instructions regarding War Diaries and Intelligence Summaries are contained in F.S. Regs., Part II. and the Staff Manual respectively. Title pages will be prepared in manuscript.

Place	Date	Hour	Summary of Events and Information	Remarks and references to Appendices
Petit Ham	1-11-18		Nothing to Report	Vet S
	2-11-18		9 animals evacuated to no 6 V.E.S.	V2b
	3-11-18		3 animal wounded & 2 to 6 V.E.S. Section moved to Renescure	V2b
Renescure	4-11-18		Nothing to Report.	V2b
	5-11-18		13 animals evacuated to No 4 V.E.S.	V2b
	6-11-18		13 animals evacuated to No 6 V.E.S. Section moved to Oremel	V2b
Oremel	7-11-18		Nothing to Report.	V2b
	8-11-18		6 animals evacuated to no 6 V.E.S. Section moved to Gonnignies	V2b
Gonnignies	9-11-18		Section moved to Bavisiau.	V2b
Bavisiau	10-11-18		Nothing to Report.	V2b
	11-11-18		Handed over to Capt Brown O.C. of 6 Mob. Vet. Sec.	V2b
			Section moved to Regt-Front	V2b
Bavisiau	11-11-18			
Regt Front	12-11-18		Nothing to report	V2b
	13-11-18		Nothing to report	V2b
	14-11-18		26 Animals evacuated to No 6 V.E.S.	V2b
	15-11-18		Nothing to report	V2b

B.O.Brown Capt AVC
O.C. 2/1 (w.R) Mob. Vet. V.S.

Army Form C. 2118.

WAR DIARY
INTELLIGENCE SUMMARY. 2/1 (W.R.) Motor Vet. Section

Original

(Erase heading not required.)

Instructions regarding War Diaries and Intelligence Summaries are contained in F. S. Regs., Part II. and the Staff Manual respectively. Title pages will be prepared in manuscript.

Place	Date	Hour	Summary of Events and Information	Remarks and references to Appendices
Surf Purrul	16.11.15		17 Animals handed to 19th D.v.V.Col.	
	17.11.15		5 Animals handed to 19th Mobile Vet Sec.	
	18.11.15		Section moved to Rouvrin	
Rouvrin	19.11.15		Section moved to Sobre-sur-Sancoure	
Sobre-sur-Sancoure	20.11.15		Section moved to Sours-sur-Huer	
	21.11.15		Nothing to report	
	22.11.15		Nothing to report	
	23.11.15		Nothing to report	
	24.11.15		Section moved to Sarcienne	
Sarcienne	25.11.15		Section moved to Hondust-Savage	
Hondust-Savage	26.11.15		Nothing to report	
	27.11.15		Section moved to Thynes	
Thynes	28.11.15		Nothing to report	
	29.11.15		Nothing to report	
	30.11.15		Nothing to report	

B.G. Major
O.C. 2/1 (W.R.) M.V.S.

Original

Confidential

SS 25

War Diary
9/8 (AR) Mobile Veterinary Section.
1st Decr 1916 to 31st Decr 1918

Volume 24

Army Form C. 2118.

Original

WAR DIARY
or
INTELLIGENCE SUMMARY.

(Erase heading not required.) of No 1 (W.R.) Mob. Veterinary Section

Instructions regarding War Diaries and Intelligence Summaries are contained in F. S. Regs., Part II. and the Staff Manual respectively. Title pages will be prepared in manuscript.

Place	Date	Hour	Summary of Events and Information	Remarks and references to Appendices
Ypres	1.12.15		Nothing to report	A/3
"	2.12.15		Nothing to report	A/3
"	3.12.15		Nothing to report	A/3
"	4.12.15		Two animals evacuated to No 9 V.E.S	A/3
"	5.12.15		Nothing to report	A/3
"	6.12.15		Nothing to report	A/3
"	7.12.15		Two animals evacuated to No 9 V.E.S	A/3
"	8.12.15		One animal evacuated to No 9 V.E.S	A/3
"	9.12.15		Nothing to report	A/3
"	10.12.15		Section moved to Loignon	A/3
Loignon	11.12.15		Section moved to Porcheresse	A/3
Porcheresse	12.12.15		Section moved to Clairie	A/3
Clairie	13.12.15		Section moved to Till	A/3
Till	14.12.15		Section moved to Rahier	A/3
Rahier	15.12.15		Nothing to report	A/3
"	16.12.15		Section moved to Petit Cor	A/3
Petit Cor	17.12.15		Section moved to Wicquinquin. Handed over to Capt Craik R.A.V.C.	A/3

Army Form C. 2118.

WAR DIARY
or
INTELLIGENCE SUMMARY.

Original
(Erase heading not required.) 2/(WR) Mobile Veterinary Section

Instructions regarding War Diaries and Intelligence Summaries are contained in F. S. Regs., Part II. and the Staff Manual respectively. Title pages will be prepared in manuscript.

Place	Date	Hour	Summary of Events and Information	Remarks and references to Appendices
Weisnes	18-12-18		Resumed Command of Section	JRG
"	19-12-18		Nothing to report.	JRG
"	20-12-18		Nothing to report.	JRG
Elsenborn	21-12-18		Section moved to Elsenborn Lager	JRG
Kalter Herberg	22-12-18		Section moved to Kalter Herberg	JRG
Herhahn	23-12-18		Section moved to Herhahn	JRG
"	24-12-18		Nothing to report.	JRG
Kalterwick	25-12-18		Section moved to Kalterwick	JRG
"	26-12-18		Nothing to report.	JRG
"	27-12-18		Nothing to report.	JRG
"	28-12-18		Nothing to report.	JRG
"	29-12-18		Nothing to report.	JRG
"	30-12-18		Nothing to report.	JRG
"	31-12-18		Nothing to report.	JRG

J.R. Grubb
Capt. R.A.V.C.
O.C. 2/(WR) M.V.S.

Confidential

War Diary
of
2/3 NZ Mobile Veterinary Section

1st Jan 1919 to 31st Jan 1919

Volume 25

(6414) Wt. W3906/P1607 2,500,000 7/18 McA & W Ltd (E 3591) Forms W3091/4.   Army Form W.3091.

Cover for Documents.

Nature of Enclosures.

Notes, or Letters written.

Army Form C. 2118.

WAR DIARY
INTELLIGENCE SUMMARY.
(Erase heading not required.)

of 2/1 (W.R) Mobile Veterinary Section

Instructions regarding War Diaries and Intelligence Summaries are contained in F. S. Regs., Part II. and the Staff Manual respectively. Title pages will be prepared in manuscript.

Place	Date	Hour	Summary of Events and Information	Remarks and references to Appendices
Keldwick	1-1-19		Nothing to report.	Ich
January	2-1-19		Nothing to report.	M.R.E.
"	3-1-19		Nothing to report.	M.R.E.
"	4-1-19		Nothing to report.	M.R.E.
"	5-1-19		Nothing to report.	M.R.E.
"	6-1-19		19 animals evacuated to No 9 V.E.S.	M.R.E.
"	7-1-19		Two animals evacuated to No 9 V.E.S.	M.R.E.
"	8-1-19		Nothing to report.	M.R.E.
"	9-1-19		Nothing to report.	M.R.E.
"	10-1-19		Nothing to report.	M.R.E.
"	11-1-19		Nothing to report.	M.R.E.
"	12-1-19		Nothing to report.	M.R.E.
"	13-1-19		11 animals evacuated to No 9 V.E.S.	M.R.E.
"	14-1-19		Nothing to report.	M.R.E.
"	15-1-19		Nothing to report.	M.R.E.

F.R Stubb
Capt. R.A.V.C.
O.C 2/1 (W.R) Mobile Veterinary Section

Army Form C. 2118.

WAR DIARY
— of —
INTELLIGENCE SUMMARY.

Page 2

(Erase heading not required.) No. 9/1 (N.R) British Veterinary Section.

Instructions regarding War Diaries and Intelligence Summaries are contained in F. S. Regs., Part II. and the Staff Manual respectively. Title pages will be prepared in manuscript.

Place	Date	Hour	Summary of Events and Information	Remarks and references to Appendices
Rödewisch	16-1-19		Nothing to report	
Germany	17-1-19		10 animals evacuated to No 9 V.E.S	F.R.b
"	18-1-19		Nothing to report	F.R.b
"	19-1-19		Nothing to report.	F.R.b
"	20-1-19		50 Class D and D- animals sent to Abteilung Cologne.	F.R.b
"	21-1-19		Nothing to report	F.R.b
"	22-1-19		Nothing to report	F.R.b
"	23-1-19		12 Class D animals sent to Abteilung Cologne.	F.R.b
"	24-1-19		Nothing to report	F.R.b
"	25-1-19		Nothing to report	F.R.b
"	26-1-19		Nothing to report.	F.R.b
"	27-1-19		Nothing to report	F.R.b
"	28-1-19		Nothing to report.	F.R.b
"	29-1-19		Nothing to report.	F.R.b
"	30-1-19		Sergt Thornton departed on leave to U.K. Pte Hawthorn reported from No 2 Veterinary hospital.	F.R.b
"	31-1-19		Nothing to report	F.R.b

F.R. Croft
F.R. Croft Capt R.A.V.C.
o.c. 9/ (N.R) Mobile Veterinary Section.

Confidential

War Diary

of

2/8 (G.R) Mobile Vet. Sect.

1 Feb 1919 to 28th Feb 1919

Volume 26

Original

Army Form C. 2118.

WAR DIARY
INTELLIGENCE SUMMARY.

(Erase heading not required.) 2/1 (W.R) Mobile Veterinary Section

Instructions regarding War Diaries and Intelligence
Summaries are contained in F. S. Regs., Part II.
and the Staff Manual respectively. Title pages
will be prepared in manuscript.

Place	Date	Hour	Summary of Events and Information	Remarks and references to Appendices
Ketsmich	1-2-19		Nothing to report	
Germany	2-2-19		Nothing to report	
	3-2-19		2 animals evacuated to No 9 V.E.S.	
	4-2-19		Nothing to report	
	5-2-19		1 animal evacuated to No 9 V.E.S. & Pte Fawcett returned to Base Tbl	
	6-2-19		Nothing to report	
	7-2-19		5 animals evacuated to No 9 V.E.S.	
	8-2-19		Nothing to report	
	9-2-19		Nothing to report	
	10-2-19		Nothing to report	
	11-2-19		5 animals evacuated to No 9 V.E.S.	
	12-2-19		No 161496 Pte Lumley J. granted 14 days special leave to U.K. Handed over command of 2/1 (W.R) M.V.S. to Captain Williams R.A.V.C. and took over duties of D.A.D.V.S.	
	13-2-19		One horse evacuated to No 9 V.E.S.	SS316 04
	14-2-19		Six animals evacuated to No 9 V.E.S.	

MR Williams
Capt RAVC
O/C 2/1 (W.R) Mobile Veterinary Section

Army Form C. 2118.

Original

WAR DIARY
or
INTELLIGENCE SUMMARY.

(Erase heading not required.) 2/1 (W.R.) Mobile Veterinary Section

Instructions regarding War Diaries and Intelligence Summaries are contained in F. S. Regs., Part II. and the Staff Manual respectively. Title pages will be prepared in manuscript.

Place	Date	Hour	Summary of Events and Information	Remarks and references to Appendices
Holdmich	15-2-19		One animal evacuated to No 9 N.E.S and Pte Richardson R.C.S granted fourteen days leave to U.K.	WRW
Germany	16-2-19		Pte Taylor A.S granted fourteen days leave to U.K.	WRW
	17-2-19		Nothing to report	WRW
	18-2-19		One animal evacuated to No 9 N.E.S and Cpl Mullarkin H.L returned from leave U.K.	WRW
	19-2-19		Nothing to report	WRW
	20-2-19		Nothing to report	WRW
	21-2-19		Three animals evacuated to No 9 N.E.S	WRW
	22-2-19		Nothing to report	WRW
	23-2-19		Nothing to report	WRW
	24-2-19		Four animals evacuated to No 9 N.E.S	WRW
	25-2-19		Nothing to report	WRW
	26-2-19		Four animals evacuated to No 9 N.E.S	WRW
	27-2-19		One animal evacuated to No 9 N.E.S	WRW
	28-2-19		Nothing to report	WRW

W.R Williams,
Capt. A.V.C
O.C 2/1 (W.R) Mobile Veterinary Section

Confidential

War Diary
2nd Vol. Original Hyla
2/1 (WR) Mobile Veterinary Section.

for
March 1919

Volume III
No III

D.K. Craib Capt RAVC
O.C. 2/1 (WR) M.V.S

Army Form C. 2118.

WAR DIARY
or
INTELLIGENCE SUMMARY.
(Erase heading not required.)

Vol: 8 *Original*

By A.R. Nott Veterinary Officer

Instructions regarding War Diaries and Intelligence Summaries are contained in F.S. Regs., Part II. and the Staff Manual respectively. Title pages will be prepared in manuscript.

Place	Date	Hour	Summary of Events and Information	Remarks and references to Appendices
Aldershot	1-3-19		105 animals evacuated to No 9 V.E.S.H. Corporal Dutton W.A.C. on leave to U.K. 10am	Apx 103
"	2-3-19		Two animals evacuated to No 9 V.E.S.	
"	3-3-19		Six animals evacuated to No 9 V.E.S. Pte Farley G returned from leave 10am	1741
"	4-3-19		Nothing to report. Captain Ackles V.E. returned on leave 11/15	1823
"	5-3-19		Nothing to report.	1726
"	6-3-19		9 animals evacuated to the 9 V.E.S.	1726
"	7-3-19		Nothing to report.	1726
"	8-3-19		22 N to report.	272.6
"	9-3-19		Nothing to report.	1726
"	10-3-19		Major Nicolson left on leave for U.K.	2723
"	11-3-19		Nothing to report.	1726
"	12-3-19		2 animals evacuated to No 9 V.E.S.	1726
"	13-3-19		Nothing to report.	1726
"	14-3-19		10 animals evacuated to No 9 V.E.S.	1726
"	15-3-19		Nothing to report.	2726
"	16-3-19		Nothing to report.	1726

Army Form C. 2118.

WAR DIARY
or
INTELLIGENCE SUMMARY.

(Erase heading not required.)

Original

2/1 (W.R.) Mobile Veterinary Section

Place	Date	Hour	Summary of Events and Information	Remarks and references to Appendices
Belluno	17-3-19		Cpl Dobbs returned from leave.	
	18-3-19		36 7 D animals and 8 Italian Cliques Phlegmon injected F.E.B.	F.E.B.
	19-3-19		Nothing to report	F.E.B.
	20-3-19		8 animals evacuated to No 2 V.E.P.	F.E.B.
	21-3-19		Nothing to report	F.E.B.
	22-3-19		Nothing to report	F.E.B.
	23-3-19		Nothing to report	F.E.B.
	24-3-19		One 7.D. transferred from M.S.C. to Demobilisation Camp Duesen	F.E.B.
	25-3-19		1 animal evacuated to No 9 V.E.S.	F.E.B.
	26-3-19		Nothing to report	F.E.B.
	27-3-19		Pte Ferguson admitted to hospital	F.E.B.
	28-3-19		Sgt Nielson reported from leave	F.E.B.
	29-3-19		Pte Boswell M.M. demobilised 6 animals evacuated to 29 V.E.S.	F.E.B.
	30-3-19		Pte Byerite departed on leave to U.K.	F.E.B.
	31-3-19		6 animals evacuated to No 9 V.E.S. Pte Murrell on leave to U.K.	F.E.B.

F.R. Charles Capt. A.V.C. (W.R.) M.V.S.

O.C. 2/1 (W.R.) M.V.S.

Confidential

War Diary

of

21st Mobile Veterinary Section (N.Z.)

from 1st May 1919 to 31st May 1919.

Army Form C. 2118.

WAR DIARY
or
INTELLIGENCE SUMMARY.
(Erase heading not required.)

2/1 (W.R.) Mobile Vety Section

Instructions regarding War Diaries and Intelligence Summaries are contained in F.S. Regs., Part II. and the Staff Manual respectively. Title pages will be prepared in manuscript.

Place	Date	Hour	Summary of Events and Information	Remarks and references to Appendices
Soller	1.5.19	—	11 Animals Evacuated to No 4 V.E.H. — Sgt Hill reported from leave	MMC
	2.5.19	—	1 Animal Evacuated to No 4 V.E.H.	MMC
	3.5.19	—	Nothing to Report	MMC
	4.5.19	—	Nothing to Report	MMC
	5.5.19	—	Nothing to Report	MMC
	6.5.19	—	1 Mule for duty from No 24 Vet. Hospital — three Evacuated to No 4 V.E.H.	MMC
	7.5.19	—	Nothing to Report	MMC
	8.5.19	—	Nothing to Report	MMC
	9.5.19	—	Nothing to Report	MMC
	10.5.19	—	Driver Shepard left unit for U.K. (Electric Cars)	MMC
	11.5.19	—	Nothing to Report	MMC
	12.5.19	—	Evacuated 20 Animals to No 4 V.C.J.	MMC
	13.5.19	—	Nothing to Report	MMC
	14.5.19	—	Nothing to Report	MMC
	15.5.19	—	Nothing to Report	MMC
	16.5.19	—	Nothing to Report	MMC

Army Form C. 2118.

WAR DIARY
or
INTELLIGENCE SUMMARY.
(Erase heading not required.)

Instructions regarding War Diaries and Intelligence Summaries are contained in F. S. Regs., Part II. and the Staff Manual respectively. Title pages will be prepared in manuscript.

Place	Date	Hour	Summary of Events and Information	Remarks and references to Appendices
Soller	17.5.19	—	S/Sergt Price reported for duty	AMC
	18.5.19	—	S/Sergt Turner left unit for U.K. (Farriers Leave)	AMC
	19.5.19	—	Nothing to Report	AMC
	20.5.19	—	Pte Donaldson & Laird reported for duty from 1/6 Black Watch	AMC
	21.5.19	—	Evacuated 1 horse to No 4 V.S.I.	AMC
	22.5.19	—	Evacuated 8 horses to No 4 V.S.I.	AMC
	23.5.19	—	Evacuated 2 horses to No 4 V.S.I.	AMC
	24.5.19	—	Nothing to Report	AMC
	25.5.19	—	Nothing to Report	AMC
	26.5.19	—	Nothing to Report	AMC
	27.5.19	—	Capt. Preston took charge of Section - Pte Williams on leave to U.K.	AMC
			Pte McGough for duty from 52nd Garden Coln.	AMC
	28.5.19	—	Lieut Crawford Rft Section for 240 Bgde R.F.A.	AMC
	29.5.19	—	Pte Shepherd & Pte Taylor reported to Section for duty	AMC
	30.5.19	—	Sergt Hill demobilised - 2 horses evacuated to No 4 V.S.I.	AMC
	31.5.19	—	Pte Sewell demobilised - 6 horses evacuated to No 4 V.S.I.	AMC

W.H. Preston
Capt. RAVC
O.C. 2/1 West Riding M.V.S. Highland Division

21st M.V.S
June 19

Confidential

War Diary

of

2/1 (W.R.) Mobile Vety Section

From 1.6.19 — To 30.6.19

(Volume XXX)

Army Form C. 2118.

WAR DIARY
or
INTELLIGENCE SUMMARY.
(Erase heading not required.)

2/(h.R) Notts (city Section)

Instructions regarding War Diaries and Intelligence Summaries are contained in F. S. Regs., Part II. and the Staff Manual respectively. Title pages will be prepared in manuscript.

Place	Date	Hour	Summary of Events and Information	Remarks and references to Appendices
Soller	1.6.19		Nothing to Report	initial
	2.6.19		Nothing to Report	initial
	3.6.19		Pte J Laud for duty from 9th Batt Leopoldo Hllo pending transfer to RAVC	initial
	4.6.19		Nothing to Report	initial
	5.6.19		Nothing to Report	initial
	6.6.19		Cpl Cooley & J Smith Brown for duty from No 2 Vet Hospital to complete establishment	initial
	7.6.19		Pte Nelson, Finnis, Tonkin & Goss for duty from 5th Batt Laicaine Hllo pending transfer to RAVC	initial
			Pte Short left unit for leave to U.K.	
			Pte Smith Douch returned to No 24 Vet Hospital for duty relieved by Smith Brown	
			Driver Nelson 525 Coy RASC (att 2/(h.R) NYE) reported at Dover for demobilisation	
	8.6.19		Nothing to Report	initial
	9.6.19		Nothing to Report	initial
	10.6.19		Pte McLaren & Lawson for duty from 10th Batt Argyll & Sutherland Hllo from 10th bag pending transfer to RAVC	initial
SOLLER	10.6.19	14.15	Riding School for attached men, who are being trained with a view to transfer to RAVC	initial

Kinner

WHR

Army Form C. 2118.

WAR DIARY
or
INTELLIGENCE SUMMARY.
(Erase heading not required.)

Unit _2/1 (W.R.) Mobile Vety Section_

Instructions regarding War Diaries and Intelligence Summaries are contained in F. S. Regs., Part II. and the Staff Manual respectively. Title pages will be prepared in manuscript.

Place	Date	Hour	Summary of Events and Information	Remarks and references to Appendices
Lillers – Germany	11.6.19	–	Pte Shepherd – R.A.S.C. driver – admitted to hospital. 13 Animals admitted to M.V.S. – 1 Animal returned to unit for duty. Pte Weston proceeded to Cologne on 4 days pass to British Empire Leave Club. Riding drill for attached Men to be transferred to R.A.V.C.	nil
"	12.6.19	–	8 Animals evacuated to No 4 V.E.D. – 2 Animals to M.V.S. sick. Sergeant Haveringham admitted to hospital. Attached Men lectured for 1 hour and 1 hour riding drill. Pte Williams reported to unit from 14 days leave to U.K.	nil
"	13.6.19	–	2 Animals admitted to M.V.S. Attached Men lectured for 1 hour and riding-drill. Pte Shepherd reported to Unit from hospital.	nil
"	14.6.19	–	Pte D. Rooney appointed to rank of Corporal with pay to complete war establishment of unit. A/Cpl Cummings and Pte Taylor reported for duty from 8th Block. Watch with a view of transfer to R.A.V.C.	nil
"	15.6.19	–	Pte Weston returned from 4 days Cologne leave.	nil
"	16.6.19	–	Cpl Rooney proceeded to M.K. on 14 days leave. Attached men lectured for 1 hour and 1 hour riding-drill.	nil

W.N.P.

Army Form C. 2118.

WAR DIARY
or
INTELLIGENCE SUMMARY.
(Erase heading not required.)

Unit 2/(Cst. R.) Mob. Vet. Section

Instructions regarding War Diaries and Intelligence Summaries are contained in F. S. Regs., Part II. and the Staff Manual respectively. Title pages will be prepared in manuscript.

Place	Date	Hour	Summary of Events and Information	Remarks and references to Appendices
Lillers	17.6.19	—	Sergt. Heveringham reported to unit from hospital.	—
Lernay			Pte Stevens left unit for 4 days furlough base. Riding drill for attached men and 1 hour lecture – Pte Club admitted to M.S.	—
"	18.6.19	—	6 Strays sent to 4th Corps Animal Collecting Camp – Doers. 5 Animals evacuated to No 4 V.E.L. and 2 Animals evacuated by Battalion on	—
"	19.6.19	—	3 Animals admitted to M.V.S.	—
"	20.6.19	—	Sergt. Griffiths reported for duty from No 7 Vet Hospital. Riding drill and 1 hour lecture for attached men. 3 Animals admitted to M.V.S.	—
"	21.6.19	—	Pte Heaton proceeded on 14 days leave to U.K. 2 Animals admitted to M.V.S.	—
"	22.6.19	—	Nothing to Report.	—
"	23.6.19	—	6 Animals admitted to M.V.S. – Riding drill for attached men. Capt. Preston handed over duties of D.A.D.V.S. to Major Verney D.S.O. who returned from temporary duties as D.A.D.V.S.	—
"	24.6.19	—	Riding drill for attached men and 1 hour lecture 2 Animals admitted to M.V.S.	—
"	25.6.19	—	8 Animals evacuated to No 4 V.E.L. Pte Marth proceeded on 14 days leave to U.K.	2 DYS IV Corps

W.H.P.

Army Form C. 2118.

WAR DIARY
or
INTELLIGENCE SUMMARY.
(Erase heading not required.)

Unit 2/1 (W.R.) Mobile Vety Section.

Instructions regarding War Diaries and Intelligence Summaries are contained in F. S. Regs., Part II. and the Staff Manual respectively. Title pages will be prepared in manuscript.

Place	Date	Hour	Summary of Events and Information	Remarks and references to Appendices
Lillers	26.6.19		Riding drill for attached men with a view to transfer to R.A.V.C.	
Germany	27.6.19		3 Animals admitted to Section	
"	28.6.19		3 Animals evacuated to No. 4 V.E.S.	
			Riding drill for attached men	
"	29.6.19		4 Animals admitted to M.V.S. Riding drill for attached men	
"	30.6.19		5 Animals admitted to M.V.S.	
			Captain W.H. Priston taken over duties of D.A.D.V.S. from Major Young D.S.O. who has been granted 14 days leave to U.K.	

W.H. Priston
Capt. R.A.V.C.

2/1st (W.R.)
MOBILE VETERINARY
SECTION.
No. M.V/97.4
Date 7.P.9

XXX

Confidential

War - Diary

of

2/1 (W.R) Mobile Vety Section

From 1. 7. 19   To 31. 7. 19

Army Form C. 2118.

WAR DIARY
or
INTELLIGENCE SUMMARY.

(Erase heading not required.)

Unit 2/1 (W.R.) Mobile Vety Section

Instructions regarding War Diaries and Intelligence Summaries are contained in F.S. Regs., Part II. and the Staff Manual respectively. Title pages will be prepared in manuscript.

Place	Date	Hour	Summary of Events and Information	Remarks and references to Appendices
Letter	1.7.19	—	Pte Ferguson granted 14 days leave to the U.K. Capt H.H. Proctor's Charger taken on section strength from No 5 B.R.D. Calais. — 1 Animal admitted to M.V.S. from Hdqrs Highland Division.	WIT
Germany	2.7.19	—	Pte Bateman granted 14 days leave to U.K. and Pte E. Brighton granted 10 days leave to France. — 1 Animal died admitted from 310 Bgde R.F.A. — 2 Animals evacuated to No 4 V.E.S. — 1 Animal returned to 10th Argyll & Sutherland Hldrs fit for duty	WIT
"	3.7.19	—	Sergt. H. Mulliken granted 14 days leave to U.K. — Pte D. Taylor attached from 8th Batt Black Watch. awarded 7 days C.B. for insolence and disobeying an order given by an N.C.O. Pte P. Short — R.A.V.C. — 1 Animal evacuated 28 days F.P. No 2 for evacuating leave to U.K.	WIT
Krem			fit for duty. — 1 Animal returned to B/310 and 1 to B/312 fit for duty	
"	6.7.19	—	1 Animal admitted to all S.L. from B/312 Bgde R.F.A. Pte T Theakston granted 14 days leave to U.K. — Pte K. Bain returned to 526 Coy R.A.P.C. temporarily attached as cover	WIT

Army Form C. 2118.

WAR DIARY
or
INTELLIGENCE SUMMARY.
(Erase heading not required.)

Instructions regarding War Diaries and Intelligence Summaries are contained in F. S. Regs., Part II. and the Staff Manual respectively. Title pages will be prepared in manuscript.

Place	Date	Hour	Summary of Events and Information	Remarks and references to Appendices
Sollen - Germany	5.7.19	—	Bathing Parade for all Ranks – 2 Stray Mules admitted to M.V.S. from 1st Highland Bgde Headquarters	WWW
"	6.7.19	—	Man attached to M.V.S. with a view to transfer returned for 1 hour. – 1 Animal collected by ambulance from Hdqrs High'd 2d Div	WWW
"	7.7.19	—	M.V.S. Inspected by D.V.S. Army of the Rhine	WWW
"	8.7.19	—	Pte Weston returned to Unit from leave – 1 Animal admitted to M.V.S. from Hdqrs 5th Tank Bgde – Riding drill for men attached with view to transfer. 1 Animal transferred to Hdqrs Highland Division fit for duty.	WWW
"	9.7.19	—	Riding drill for attached men – 1 Animal collected by ambulance from 526 Bay R.A.S.C. – 1 Animal admitted from Hdqrs/310 Bgde R.F.A.	WWW
"	10.7.19	—	Pte K. Month reported to unit from leave. 1 Animal admitted to M.V.S. from A/312 Bgde R.F.A. – 1 from No 2 Section D.A.C. and 2 from 460 Field Coy R.E	WWW
"	11.7.19	—	Bathing Parade for all ranks. – Attached men returned for 1 hour.	WWW

Army Form C. 2118.

WAR DIARY
or
INTELLIGENCE SUMMARY.
(Erase heading not required.)

Instructions regarding War Diaries and Intelligence Summaries are contained in F.S. Regs., Part II. and the Staff Manual respectively. Title pages will be prepared in manuscript.

Place	Date	Hour	Summary of Events and Information	Remarks and references to Appendices
Sellers	12.7.19	—	Ptes Brighton & Mantle reported from leave. — 1 Animal returned to 5.25 Coy R.A.S.C. fit for duty. — 1 Animal admitted to M.V.S.	Appx
Gercay			from Hdqrs 3rd Highland Bgde. — 1 from Hdqrs 1/312 Bgde R.F.A. and 1 from L.A.A. Section Highland D.A.C.	
"	13.7.19	—	Rifle & Saddlery Inspection. — 1 Animal collected by ambulance from 10th Argyll & Sutherland Hldrs. — 2 Animals admitted from C/310 Bgde R.F.A. — 3 Animals evacuated to No 4 V.E.L. and 1 returned to A/312 Bgde R.F.A. fit for duty.	Appx
"	14.7.19	—	1 Animal collected by ambulance from Highland Division M.M.P's Attached men lectured for 1 hour on Wound "dressing".	Appx
"	15.7.19	—	2 stray mules evacuated to No 4 Animal Collecting Camp. Cpl Coley R.A.V.C. granted 14 days leave to U.K. & Sergt Griffin instructed to report to No 4 Vety Hospital Calais for duty. 2 Animals admitted to M.V.S. from 8th Batt Black Watch. 3 Animals evacuated to No 4 Vety Evacuating Station	Appx

… Army Form C. 2118.

WAR DIARY
or
INTELLIGENCE SUMMARY.

(Erase heading not required.)

Instructions regarding War Diaries and Intelligence Summaries are contained in F. S. Regs., Part II. and the Staff Manual respectively. Title pages will be prepared in manuscript.

Place	Date	Hour	Summary of Events and Information	Remarks and references to Appendices
Solbes	16.7.19		Capt M.H. Priston handed over duties of D.A.D.V.S. to Major Verny D.S.O. who returned off leave from U.K.	
Germany			1 Animal returned to H.Q./310 Bgde R.F.A. Fit for duty & returned to 460 Field Coy. Medical Inspection for all ranks by M.O. Highland Div School of Musketry	
"	17.7.19		Pte Ferguson returned from leave from U.K. - 1 Animal returned to duty to 9/312 Bgde R.F.A.	
"	18.7.19		Pte Bateman returned from leave from U.K. Attached allow Lectured for 1 hour. - 4 Animals admitted to M.V.S. from A/310 Bgde R.F.A. - Y.1 from B/312 Bgde R.F.A	
"	19.7.19		Riding drill for attached men - half days holiday. 3 Animals evacuated to No. 4 V.E.S.	
"	20.7.19		A.D.V.S. visited & Inspected M.V.S.	
"	21.7.19		Capt M.H. Priston visited sick animal suffering from Enteritis at Hdqrs 3rd Highland Bgde.	

Army Form C. 2118.

WAR DIARY
or
INTELLIGENCE SUMMARY.
(Erase heading not required.)

Instructions regarding War Diaries and Intelligence Summaries are contained in F. S. Regs., Part II. and the Staff Manual respectively. Title pages will be prepared in manuscript.

Place	Date	Hour	Summary of Events and Information	Remarks and references to Appendices
Lillers	21.7.19		All animals in M.V.S. re-classified by D.A.D.V.S. and Animal Classification Committee. - 1 Animal returned to 526 Coy R.A.S.C. fit for duty. - 2 Animals admitted from 310 Bgde R.F.A	
Gemery	22.7.19		3 Animals admitted to M.V.S. from 6th Batt Black Watch. 5 Animals evacuated to No 4 V.E.L. - 1 Animal admitted from 52nd Gordons Hldrs and 1 from 525 Coy R.A.S.C. Collected by Ambulance. Capt Prior inspected animals of 8th Batt Black Watch. Post Mortem held on horse that died at 3rd Highland Bgde Hdqrs death due to ruptured colon after recovered in M.V.S.	
"	23.7.19		Lieut McMaster returned from leave from U.K. - 2 Animals evacuated to No 4 V.E.L. and D.A.D.V.S inspected M.V.S.	
"	24.7.19		3 Animals evacuated to No 4 V.E.L. and 1 by ambulance.	
"	25.7.19		Bathing Parade for all ranks General of Unit paid by O.C. 1 Animal returned to Hdqrs 1/310 Bde. R.F.A fit for duty	
"	26.7.19		1 T" Mule evacuated to No 4 Animal Collecting Camp Capt Prior visited M.M.9 Horse for D.A.D.M. Highland Division.	

Army Form C. 2118.

WAR DIARY
or
INTELLIGENCE SUMMARY.
(Erase heading not required.)

Instructions regarding War Diaries and Intelligence Summaries are contained in F. S. Regs., Part II. and the Staff Manual respectively. Title pages will be prepared in manuscript.

Place	Date	Hour	Summary of Events and Information	Remarks and references to Appendices
Lother	27.7.19		Nothing to Report	
Germany	28.7.19		Nothing to Report	
"	29.7.19		Nothing to Report	
"	30.7.19		1 Animal Returned to 8th Batt Black Watch fit for duty	
"	31.7.19		Medical Inspection for all ranks by M.O. Instead of Inhability Cpl Lacky R.A.V.C returned from leave from U.K.	

W. M. Renton
Capt RAVC

Original.

Confidential

War Diary

of

2/1(H.R.)Mob'l Vety Section

Highland Division

From - 1.8.19 — To - 30.8.19.

Army Form C. 2118.

WAR DIARY
or
INTELLIGENCE SUMMARY.
(Erase heading not required.)

Place	Date	Hour	Summary of Events and Information	Remarks and references to Appendices
Sutton	1-8-19		At established 461 Field Company R.G.A. Funeral Cortege. 2 Animals admitted to M.V.S. from 52" Bgde. Bathing Parties & Weeks	WDP 19
Germany	2-8-19		Nothing to Report.	WDP
"	3-8-19		Nothing to Report.	WDP
"	4-8-19		1 Animal admitted to M.V.S. from 526 Coy. R.L.C.	WDP
"	5-8-19		16 Officers returned from leave. 3 Animals admitted from Hedgeralis Highland Division	WDP
"			2 Animals discharged to Ingerton Highland Division. 1 Animal discharged to 1st Highland Brigade	WDP
"	6-8-19		1 Animal admitted to Pvt V.Sd. by Heat.	WDP
"			1 Animal evacuated to Pvt V.Sd. by Heat. M.M.P.	WDP
"	7-8-19		1 Animal admitted to M.V.S. from School of Musketry. 17 Animals evacuated to the 4 V.Sd. (15 horses 2 mules)	WDP
"	8-8-19		15 Establishment horses handed to 4" Corps A.C.C. 4 Animals handed to 4" Corps A.C.C for duty.	WDP
"	9-8-19		Station entrained at Dover for journey to England. Left Battn HC + 8 Other Ranks went to Cologne	WDP
"			with horses.	
"	10-8-19		Nothing to Report.	WDP
"	11-8-19		Lecture. Left Calais and landed at Folkestone, proceeded to Thorncliffe + entrained for Cupartins Camp.	WDP
Cupartins Camp	12-8-19		Arrived at Clipstone Camp. Batt under Station Command.	WDP
"	13-8-19		Nothing to Report.	WDP
"	14-8-19		Nothing to Report.	WDP
"	15-8-19		Report of H. Boston. Left Best for 14 days leave. Period of M.V.S. trial by Camp Commandant	WDP
"			Private Taylor T and Private Morrow J. Guiety received conviction ticket.	WDP
"	16-8-19		Nothing to Report.	WDP

Army Form C. 2118.

WAR DIARY
or
INTELLIGENCE SUMMARY.
(Erase heading not required.)

Instructions regarding War Diaries and Intelligence Summaries are contained in F. S. Regs., Part II. and the Staff Manual respectively. Title pages will be prepared in manuscript.

Place	Date	Hour	Summary of Events and Information	Remarks and references to Appendices
Whitstone Rects.	17-8-19		Nothing to Report	WYP
	18-8-19		Nothing to Report	WYP
	19-8-19		Nothing to Report	WYP
	20-8-19		Nothing to Report	WYP
	21-8-19		Nothing to Report	WYP
	22-8-19		Sgt Henningham S/S 13900 Russell, Bowell, Farley, Pizzy, Sparrow, Taylor J, Wilkins, Voyle D, Dunbar, Ford C, Laird S, Evans, Haber, York, Dunnaw, Burdan, and Cpl Hemmings? Granted 15 days leave.	WYP WYP WYP WYP WYP WYP WYP
	23-8-19		Nothing to Report	WYP
	24-8-19		Nothing to Report	WYP
	25-8-19		Nothing to Report	WYP
	26-8-19		Pte York returned to his unit.	WYP
	27-8-19		Nothing to Report	WYP
	28-8-19		Pte Thurston granted leave from 28/8/19 to 2/9/19. 14141 Pte Farley of Luneberger?	WYP
	29-8-19		No 14616 Pte Williams J. Demobilised.	WYP
	30-8-19		No 168-23 Cpl Penney 125 to 1224, Pte Abbott Demobilised Sgt Saddler B/S 13 Graham Privates and Ser. Stephens reported sick 11 times from Remount Depot Shirenampton.	WYP

W.Y.P. master
K. V.
CAPTAIN A. V. C.
O. C. 2/1 (W. R.) MOBILE VETERINARY SECTION

www.ingramcontent.com/pod-product-compliance
Lightning Source LLC
Chambersburg PA
CBHW081432160426
43193CB00013B/2255